THE DIALECTICS OF
FRIENDSHIP

THE DIALECTICS OF FRIENDSHIP

EDITED BY
ROY PORTER AND SYLVANA TOMASELLI

ROUTLEDGE
LONDON AND NEW YORK

First published 1989
by Routledge
11 New Fetter Lane, London EC4P 4EE

Simultaneously published in the USA and Canada
by Routledge
a division of Routledge, Chapman and Hall, Inc.
29 West 35th Street, New York, NY 10001

Typeset by LaserScript Limited, Mitcham, Surrey
Printed and bound in Great Britain by
Biddles Ltd, Guildford and King's Lynn

British Library Cataloguing in Publication Data
The dialectics of friendship
1. Friendship
I. Porter, Roy, 1946- II. Tomaselli, Sylvana, 1957-
302

Library of Congress Cataloging in Publication Data
The dialectics of friendship / edited by Roy Porter
and Sylvana Tomaselli
p. cm.
1. Friendship. 2. Friendship—History. I. Porter, Roy, 1946-.
II. Tomaselli, Sylvana.
BF575.F66D5 1989
177'.6—dc19
89-3510
CIP

ISBN 0-415-01751-3

CONTENTS

NOTES ON CONTRIBUTORS

Logie Barrow is Professor of Social History at the University of Bremen. He has worked extensively on the history of nineteenth-century working-class communities and socialism. His book *Independent Spirits* was published by Routledge in 1986.

Gillian Clark teaches in the Department of Classics and Archaeology at Liverpool University, and in Theological Studies at Manchester University. A book on the role of women in the later Roman Empire is forthcoming from the Clarendon Press.

Stephen R. L. Clark is Professor of Philosophy at Liverpool University. His books include *The Nature of the Beast* (OUP), on the relation of non-human to human character and behaviour; *The Mysteries of Religion* (Blackwell), on the philosophy of religion; and *Limits and Renewals* (forthcoming from Clarendon Press), a three-volume restatement of traditional approaches to society, the soul and God.

Pat Easterling is Professor of Greek at University College London. She is General Editor (with E. J. Kenney) of the series Cambridge Greek and Latin Classics and (with B. M. W. Knox) of the *Cambridge History of Classical Literature*, vol. I (1985). She has edited Sophocles' *Women of Trachis* and works mainly on Greek tragedy.

Adrian Furnham was educated at the London School of Economics where he obtained a distinction in his MSc Econ, and Oxford University where he completed a doctorate (DPhil) in 1981. Previously a lecturer in Psychology at Pembroke College, Oxford, he now teaches at University College London. He has lectured widely abroad and held scholarships at amongst others the University of New South Wales and the University of the West Indies. He has written nearly 200 scientific papers and eight books including *Culture Shock* (1986) (with S. Bochner); *The Economic Mind* (1986) (with A. Lewis); *Lay Theories* (1988) and *The Protestant Work Ethic* (forthcoming, 1989).

Stephanie Garrett is a Lecturer in Sociology at St Alban's College of Further Education. She is also a GCE A Level Sociology Examiner and Moderator. She was Head of Sociology at a London comprehensive school for ten years. She has recently completed an MA in Deviancy and Social Policy. She is author of *Gender* (Tavistock, 1987).

Margaret Kinnell lectures on childhood and children's literature at the Department of Library and Information Studies, Loughborough University. Children's books became a preoccupation through working with children as a public librarian and then teacher; several years as an antiquarian bookseller developed the fascination for early children's literature which formed the subject of her doctoral thesis. In addition to papers and an edited collection of essays, *Only the Best is Good Enough* (1985), she is managing editor of *The International Review of Children's Literature and Librarianship* and is currently researching seventeenth-century literature for children.

Sue Limb read English at Cambridge. Following an early career as a teacher, she became a freelance journalist and then a writer and broadcaster. She has written several radio scripts including *The Wordsmiths at Gorsemere*. She co-authored a biography of Captain Oates before turning to fiction. *Up the Garden Path*, her first novel, and *Love Forty*, a volume of light-hearted autobiography, are published by Corgi Books. Her work for children is published by Orchard Books.

Graham Little graduated in Economics from the University of Melbourne, was awarded a PhD in Sociology at the Australian National University before joining a programme in psychology and politics at Yale. He was appointed to the University of Melbourne's Politics Department in 1971 where he is now a Reader, teaching political psychology. Among his publications are

Political Ensembles, a psychosocial approach to politics and leadership (OUP, 1985), and *Strong Leadership: Thatcher, Reagan and an Eminent Person* (OUP, 1988).

Michael Neve lectures at the Wellcome Institute for the History of Medicine, London, and at University College London. He has recently prepared editions of Darwin's *Journal of Researches*, and of B. A. Morel's *Treatise on Degenerations* (1857).

Roy Porter read History at Christ's College, Cambridge. His PhD was published in revised form in 1977 as *The Making of Geology*. He has written and edited many books, including *The Pelican Social History of England: The Eighteenth Century* and *Revolution and History*. He lectures on The Social History of Medicine at the Wellcome Institute for the History of Medicine, London and is William Andrews Clark Professor at UCLA (1988–9).

James Serpell was awarded a degree in Zoology at University College London in 1974, and a PhD in Animal Behaviour at the University of Liverpool in 1980. At present, he is Research Associate at Cambridge University's Sub-Department of Animal Behaviour, and Director of the Cambridge Companion Animal Research Group. He has written extensively on the subject of human attitudes to, and relationships with, both wild and domestic animals, and is author of *In the Company of Animals* (Blackwell, 1986).

Sylvana Tomaselli was a research student at King's College, Cambridge, before becoming a Research Fellow of Newnham College, Cambridge (1985–8). She is an intellectual historian working predominantly on the seventeenth and eighteenth centuries. Her published work includes articles on the history of theories of personal identity and on the history of women. She has edited *Rape: an Historical and Social Enquiry* with Roy Porter.

INTRODUCTION

'Never be without a friend', proclaim the advertisements for a famous cough sweet, expressing sentiments about the cardinal importance of friendship which none of us would deny, for they are part of the established popular wisdom of our society. 'A friend in need is a friend indeed', the proverb tells us, indicating that friends are more than pleasant appendages – they attend to our deepest personal needs. A true friend is, indeed, a treasure. In the words of the sentimental popular song, 'when you've got friends and neighbours, you're the richest man in town'. Our times have been described as the age of the lonely crowd – indeed, as Logie Barrow argues, discussing a moment in the history of friendship, the life of loneliness lived amidst strangers has been perceived as a characteristic of all modern society. When in need, to whom does one turn?

Perhaps to the family. Families provide one possibility of such a support system, putatively, in Christopher Lasch's evocative phrase, a 'haven in a heartless world'. But the century of Freud, and in particular the Freudian notion of the Oedipal struggle, has dynamited the idea of 'happy families', oases of harmony free from rivalry and conflict. In any case, the reality of the 'post-modern family' – often an arena of violence and sexual abuse, and so frequently a one-parent family, an isolated atom – no longer corresponds to the conventional image of security and stability.

Another great ideal of Western society, ever since the age of Romanticism, has been the hope of finding security and fulfilment – indeed, to find *ourselves* – in love, in romantic union. Is this the institution which can meet our deepest needs? Perhaps, but culture and experience (most obviously, soaring divorce rates)

1

unite to remind us that love itself – at least in its secular form of *eros* – is crazy and unstable. The noble passion which both Romantic and romantic writers have represented in the language of dedication and sacrifice may also be a mask for the deeply selfish and often destructive drive of the libido.

If parents and lovers entangle us with relationships too fraught, too ambivalent, to meet our needs for support and company, do we then need to turn to something more formal, official, and organized? Maybe we ought to devote ourselves to the State or a Party, to a church, or a corporation, or a good cause. Yet, once again, experience may teach us to be sceptical, perhaps even cynical, about those – notoriously the 'Moonies', recently – who urge us to merge our identities into a higher cause. In his profound investigation of the psychopathology of Fascism, Wilhelm Reich suggested that identifying with the 'big men' chiefly had an appeal to inadequate 'little men' – with consequences which produced not mutuality, but authoritarian hierarchies, replicating rather than resolving the original problem. Accounts of 'corporation man' and 'organization man' are no less chilling.

These are just some of the reasons why friendship wears such an attractive face when we stretch out our hands for fellow feeling in a society which is not merely vast and anonymous, but whose self-professed ideology of the market place proclaims a 'beggar-your-neighbour' philosophy. Even the very notion of 'society' now meets with suspicion. The present British Prime Minister is on record as saying, with approval, that no such thing as 'society' exists: merely individuals and families. So if 'society' can provide no supporting community in the modern age, the role of friends becomes all the more vital. Friends are people you can rely on. Friends don't make unreasonable and excessive demands upon you. Friendship – to continue the clichés – stands for giving, not asking. Friendship does not depend on the precarious, wayward and fickle accidents of sexual attractiveness. It is not built upon the sandy foundations of a sparkle in the eyes, a jutting jaw, a shapely ankle, but upon the solid basis of mutual outlooks and shared interests. Indeed, as Stephanie Garrett shows in her essay which examines the sociology of friendship in modern Britain, people do in reality choose as friends people very much like themselves: friendship tends to be a same-sex, same-class phenomenon. This may be because we like to think that we're just the people we ourselves would choose to have as our own friends. Or, as the cynic would put it, friendship satisfies our silent conviction that if only there were more people like 'myself' around, life would be altogether more pleasant and hopeful.

That friendship contains a narcissistic element is hardly new; nor need it necessarily be seen as shameful. On the contrary, the Greeks and Romans thought it was natural that friendship should thrive amongst like-minded people (though, as Pat Easterling shows in her essay, not exclusively so), and elucidated the nature of friendship by drawing analogies with the nature of one's relation with oneself. 'When a man thinks of a true friend', wrote Cicero, in one of the most significant analyses of friendship in the Western tradition, 'he is looking at himself in the mirror'.

Making friends is always a good sign. Where there is friendship, it betokens maturity in the individual, and suggests a basic decency about the society at large. Sarah Fielding's novel, *The Adventures of David Simple* (1744), tells the tale of an innocent abroad, battling through a world in which everyone, it seems, cheats, lies, robs, exploits, and, worst of all, wears the mask of hypocrisy. Yet, by the close of the book, the hero has made himself two solid friends. With them, and his wife, and through withdrawal into a simple rural community, he manages to achieve a happiness that had always previously eluded him. Some forms of social order may, of course, be so cruel and dictatorial as altogether to preclude the possibility of friendship flourishing as an informal social institution. Sarah Fielding's contemporary, the great pioneer French sociologist, Montesquieu – the man who confessed 'Je suis amoureux de l'amitié' – designated one 'ideal type' of polity as the 'despotic'. In a despotic society, friendship could not thrive, because all social relations are based not upon positive human sentiments such as justice, honour or virtue, but upon the negative power of fear. Fear and friendship are mutually exclusive. As so often, the Greeks had got there first. In his *Nicomachean Ethics*, Aristotle tells us that 'in tyranny, there is little or no friendship.'

A certain equality makes friendship easier. The tradition of moral philosophy and social duties developed by the Greeks and elaborated by the Romans set great store, as Pat Easterling shows in her account, by friendship (*philia* was the Greek term) as an indispensable element in the good life. This, it was often stressed in Greek thought, could not be achieved between people at large, but only within certain social strata. Educated free male citizens, blessed with leisure, could exercise the virtues required for being good friends; but the Greeks did not think it natural to suppose that such men could truly join in friendship with others (slaves, artisans, women, foreigners). One could hardly be friends with those who were not one's equals. Such ideas were developed and expanded by Cicero, who believed that friends should have the same tastes and sympathies ('birds of a feather flock together', or in the modern saying, friends could be 'thick as thieves'). In time, however, a more encompassing notion of the 'equality of man' – not social but spiritual – developed, particularly with the philosophy of the Stoics. Stoic philosophers advocated disregarding social and national boundaries as artificial. Mankind was united through the common attribute, reason. Thus they created a potential for friendships to be inclusive rather than exclusive, based upon the secure foundations of 'reason' and 'humanity': *philia* became *philanthropia*.

We can see this ideal working in practice. Edward Gibbon was a rather private person. The historian of the Roman Empire never married (and, unlike certain historians and biographers, we should not leap to the conclusion that he must, therefore, have been homosexually inclined: there is no evidence for it). A man of scholarly temperament, he lived much amongst his books (sometimes he called them his friends, sometimes his 'seraglio'). Yet no one could call him solitary, still less lonely, because he had a great talent for making friends and keeping them.

Two friendships in particular spanned the bulk of his adult life. One was with the Swiss man of letters, Georges Deyverdun: between them they eventually set up house in Lausanne. The other was with John Holroyd, later Lord Sheffield, who was so good a friend as to become Gibbon's trusted literary executor. These men shared much in common – comfortable backgrounds, travelling, cosmopolitanism, an enlightened, man-of-the-world outlook upon life, literary tastes, good living. Above all, they gave each other much by way of companionship, steady moral support through times of trouble, and, not least, practical aid (once Gibbon had migrated to Switzerland, Holroyd worked like a Trojan for him in England to keep his financial affairs in good order).

But there is more to Gibbon – and to friendship – than that. He established relations with Holroyd's wife and daughter which bear all the hallmarks of friendship. After his own engagement to Suzanne Curchod was broken off, he succeeded in transforming the fractured relationship of a failed love affair into enduring friendship. Not least, he managed to turn his link with his step-mother – commonly a tie so mutually embarrassing, even hostile – into one of rich friendship. And finally, he treated all his readers as his friends. For Gibbon, friendship was the best of all relationships, and being the best of friends, the best of all human conditions. His letters show friendships which proved wonderfully serene, indeed, life-long. Sue Limb's essay provides a modern analogue. She raises at least two and a half cheers for the value of woman-to-woman friendships – lasting and mutually supportive – of the kind which Gibbon would have understood.

Personal testimonies of the need for and continued existence of real bonds of friendships endure besides sour undertones and threads of scepticism running through our common consciousness about friendship. That friends only prove themselves worthy of the name in moments of adversity is a common-place. That more often than not it is precisely those one counted on in such trials who tend to fail us is no less a frequent complaint. Bereavement, separation and divorce are the great telling points in today's Western society of the strength and trustworthiness of people's affection, whereas in centuries gone by, loss of fortune or of status were taken as the quintessential moment of revelation of true friendship as well as of romantic love. Of course the shock which we may thus have to face, so well rendered by such appellations as 'fair-weather friends', need not be taken as categorical denial of the possibility of friendship. Rather than being altogether dismissive of friendship, such a saying as 'with friends like these who needs enemies?', may just be a warning to pick our friends better. Indeed such cautionary warnings are so constitutive of our culture that, as Margaret Kinnell notes appositely, the choosing of wrong friends has been a central theme of books for children.

However, it is undeniably also the case that scepticism about friendship runs deeper than this. 'You should never trust people too much', or 'You should never expect too much of people' warn us against all, and not only 'false' or 'superficial' friends. When one calls a dog 'man's best friend', or when the singing cowboy, Roy Rogers, croons:

A four-legged friend, a four-legged friend,
He'll never let you down

it's a crown of approval for dogs and horses, but the reverse side of
the message is a thumbs-down for human friendships. For, as
Rogers goes on, 'a two-legged *hombre* is worthless as sand' – the sort
of person who'll 'promise to stick by your side like a pal,/ But he'll
also promise the same to your gal'. Jane Austen's juvenile fantasia,
Love and Freindship [sic] tells the same story. The teenage girls who
are the joint heroines are always, ever so innocently,
double-crossing each other and all their other 'friends'. 'Most
friendship is feigning', Shakespeare tells us in one of his
bittersweet songs. Perhaps the best sorts of friends, after all, are,
indeed, *Fisherman's Friends* cough pastilles.

For it seems that friendships too, like families and lovers, are
frail, fallible and fractious. Furthermore, we evidently should not
look upon them in too star-struck a light. When Mark Anthony
rises to address the Roman mob with 'Friends, Romans,
Countrymen', we are only too well aware of Shakespeare's
dramatic irony, of the contempt with which Anthony regards those
he calls his friends. The language of friendship certainly lies open
to manipulation for cynical purposes. More importantly, in traditional societies and still today, friendships have often been not so
much idealistic personal ties, but chiefly practical, down-to-earth
exchange-systems, forged for self-advancement. You designate
those people your friends, who you hope will help you get on. Even
the self-confessed lover of friendship, Montesquieu, was not too
blind to own that 'Friendship is a contract, into which we enter to
render small services to someone, so that he will do us large ones'.
Like Rousseau, he thought sincerity a scarce commodity in the
courtier society of *ancien régime* France. How could friendship exist
on any other basis than self-advantage in a society that resembled
a hall of mirrors? More recently, and in a manner which can easily
be extended to a great number of other contemporary societies,
Georg Heinrich, writing of life in Hungary today, explains that
'friendship is a mobility channel for both sexes'. Two thousand
years earlier, Cicero had deplored the fact that most people
seemed to 'choose their best friends as they choose their cattle.'

An entrepreneur in the industrial revolution, such as Matthew
Boulton, the Birmingham iron-master, thought that one of the

responsibilities of his friends was to loan him money without interest for indefinite periods, to finance his business. In Boulton's England, many of the political groupings around Parliament and the Court were known as 'Lord X's friends' or 'the King's friends'. These were patronage groupings. Attaching yourself to them was the fast-lane to career success and upward social mobility. In a society lacking structured, regular formal channels of promotion, and without reliable institutions such as banks and credit, friendship was the ladder people used to climb up society, and the safety-net preventing people from coming to too much harm when they fell.

So while friendship is not all it seems, it can also be a great deal more than it seems. Getting to the root of its nature has always been difficult and puzzling. In the early eighteenth century *The British Apollo*, a popular magazine, printed a reader's query which asked: *'What is friendship, and wherein doth it consist?'* The editor replied, *'Friendship* consists in the Perfect Union and Harmony of Souls.' This is no longer our language, and so we must ask the question once again. The essays in this book examine it closely from various points of view – psychological, theological, personal and so forth – and reveal that it constitutes a highly complex and often confusing social institution and personal commitment. As the essays on 'Friendship in the Christian tradition' and 'Freud, friendship, and politics' in particular point out, it is not even easy to work out a coherent philosophy of precisely which moral ideals or personal psychology friendship embodies. Is friendship truly altruistic? Or should it be?

Let us examine one problem, raised by Gillian and Stephen Clark. Christianity enjoins universal 'charity'. Does it follow that you *ought* to make *everyone* your friend? If that were the case, wouldn't the special quality of friendship be lost? – that notion that certain people are particularly dear and close to you. What becomes then of the idea of a 'best friend', which has sustained many a lonely childhood? Or are we perhaps unwittingly committed to the view that there is something morally reprobatory, or at least socially disturbing, about the practice of caring more for one's friends than for those we consider mere acquaintances or strangers? Moreover, in the light of the fact that we choose our friends amongst those who resemble us, who are in a meaningful sense like us, is friendship not the breeding ground for exclusiveness and privilege? If we are indeed suspicious of such societies as the Freemasons, should we not welcome the friendless world as the world in which we are open and fair to everyone and not only to some?

Nor do difficulties end here. We might question the nature of friendship from a different angle by asking if there ever can be any expectations, much less duties, in friendship when its very essence is that, unlike being part of a family, or a citizen or subject, it is a voluntary relationship which evolves often in spite of ourselves, or unknown to us. We might work with someone or simply know them socially, it seems, when all of a sudden, or perhaps just gradually, we find ourselves in a web of demands, habits and expectations. What if any are our duties then? We don't often so much choose our friends, no matter how much they might prove to resemble us, as stumble upon them. Alternatively, acquaintances turn into or are with the passage of time re-described as friends. How often do we, thanks to the passing of years, claim as school friends people whom we originally couldn't stand or whose companionship we can't even truly remember? Are such relationships necessarily more vacuous for being started or rekindled on somewhat false pretences? Indeed this line of questioning might even lead us to question the Classical view, that friends are like each other and hence like each other as they like themselves. In one of the most poignant passages in Western literature, Marcel Proust ends *Swann in Love (Un Amour de Swann)* with Swann's realization that the greatest passion of his life, the love of his life, for which he had once wanted to die, was for a woman he didn't even like, one who was not even his type. Friendships are not always that different. We do not always choose our friends in a way which would imply they are 'our type'. Bonds and relationships sometimes evolve over time such that we might act as true friends to people, assisting them in need and comforting them, without necessarily liking them. The notion that one might love but not like someone is not an unfamiliar one. Such ties might thus come closer to familial relations than to the Classical ideal of friendship.

But matters are even more complex than that. Returning to Clark and Clark's essay, we find that Christianity is fundamentally ambivalent about the 'self-love' which many like Cicero saw as the basis of friendship. Within Christianity, self-love is seen as tending towards evil, a form of vanity; yet Christians are also enjoined to model their relations to others on that which they have with themselves, to love their neighbours as themselves. Christianity thus offers complex outlooks upon friendship. Yet it does not, of course, denigrate friendship: after all, the Quakers formally call themselves the Society of Friends.

Psychoanalysis for its part, as Graham Little shows, has difficulty in resolving the dilemmas posed by the supposed altruism of the emotional bonds of friendship. Freud was disposed to see all powerful emotional attachments as driven by sexual desire. If being friends is *not* being lovers ('we are just good friends' – or what is popularly, if inaccurately, called 'platonic friendship'), then can psychoanalysis give an adequate account of friendship, except as some form of displacement or sublimation? In that case, is not friendship degraded through being reduced to and understood in terms of that which it is not?

The authors and editors of this book believe friendship plays a central part in the personal and public lives we lead. Its importance to us is so much taken for granted that it is rarely reflected upon. The prestige of psychoanalytical approaches in this century has meant that disproportionate attention has been focused upon the individual, or the individual and the nuclear family. Historians write about individuals (biographies) or societies, but less commonly about groups. Sociologists for their part have concentrated their attentions on the larger social structures. Small-scale and relatively informal communities have received less attention. This is a pity, because friendship is one of the essential pilots guiding us from childhood into adulthood, from the family into society at large.

This book raises and at least reflects upon, if it does not resolve, the great questions about friendship, by examining it from many points of view. The wider social dimensions are taken up by Logie Barrow, who focuses upon some of the meanings of friendship at an important juncture in our own history, that time of fragmentation and the dissolution of certainties towards the close of the Victorian era, and by Stephanie Garrett, who looks at friendship in our society today. The roots of the European cultural heritage are explored by Pat Easterling's discussion of Classical ideals, and by Clark and Clark, who go on to explore precisely how the Christian religion grappled with, and sought to handle, the conundrums posed by friendship in a theology in which God is Love and Love is God.

The ways in which these different but interlocking cultural heritages expressed themselves in individual cases form one of the main focuses of Margaret Kinnell's examination of children's literature. Her point that childhood was traditionally seen as the crucial period for forming friendships is in turn confirmed and further explored by Adrian Furnham's discussion of the psychology of childhood friendships and their significance for adult development – issues on which Graham Little in turn scrutinizes the answers psychoanalysts produce.

As Stephanie Garrett's essay shows, friendships are typically same-sex. The special features of female friendship and male friendship are the themes developed respectively in the contributions by Michael Neve and Sue Limb. Michael Neve argues that the very fact of admitting the need for friends is itself a valuable act of emancipation, a liberation from the macho male myth of self-sufficiency. While Sue Limb properly reminds us that if friendship has a public role, in our society its personal side is supreme.

Overall the hope of all of us involved in this book has been to stimulate thought on the part friendship has played, is playing, and ought to be playing in our culture. How highly do we prize friendship? What do we expect of it? How will it develop? In a world of dissolving certainties and intense psycho-social pressures, pondering these questions may help us with strategies for survival.

REFERENCES

The individual essays in this book contain their own notes of relevant books. The following focus upon the broad area covered by this book.

Blum, L. A. (1980) *Friendship, Altruism and Morality*, London: Routledge & Kegan Paul.

Brain, R. (1976) *Friends and Lovers*, London: Hart-Davis, MacGibbon.

Hutter, H. (1978) *Politics as Friendship: The Origins of Classical Notions of Politics and the Practice of Friendship*, Waterloo, Ontario.

Leyton, E. (ed.) (1974) *The Compact: Selected Dimensions of Friendship*, Memorial University of Newfoundland, Newfoundland Social and Economic Papers, no. 3.

Chapter One

FRIENDSHIP AND THE GREEKS

PAT EASTERLING

The ancient Greeks had a word for most things; in fact they had several that we regularly and more or less accurately translate as 'friend'. But they had no word that covered exactly the same ground as 'friend' does in our culture. *Philos*, the commonest and widest-ranging of all the Greek terms, was applied, when used as a noun, to any of one's 'nearest and dearest', irrespective of whether they were kin, affines, or other people unrelated by blood, with whom one had personal or familial ties. Used as an adjective *philos* meant 'dear'; in our earliest texts its meaning often oscillates between 'dear' and 'own' (see Hooker 1987 for discussion of the word's history). This suggests the fundamental importance and value of having people one could call one's *philoi* (plural): being *aphilos* (without a *philos*) is imagined as a desperate plight, as bad as being *apolis* (without a city). But we should not fall into the trap of treating the relationship too sentimentally: it was based, after all, on the assumption that a person's *philos*-network came largely ready-made. There was little obvious room for spontaneity, freedom of choice, personal likes and dislikes in a culture where your *philoi* included all your kin and the closest of *their philoi*; and it is perhaps not surprising that Greek literature often deals with the problem of defining just who one's *philoi* are.

Plays like Sophocles' *Electra* and *Ajax* explore what happens when people who ought to be *philoi* start behaving like enemies: when Clytemnestra has killed her husband her children are faced with an insoluble dilemma, since to do the right thing as *philoi* of their father means behaving as enemies to their mother, and when Ajax tries to kill the comrades who have profoundly insulted him, his problem, which he resolves only by suicide, is seen in terms of

11

philos-relationships. In our culture it is kin relationships (or sexual ones) that are particularly associated with the extremes of love and hate; in Greek culture the same intensity is attributed to a differently defined nexus of human associations.

The word most commonly used as the opposite of *philos* is *echthros*, more easily translatable as 'enemy' than *philos* is as 'friend'. Greek ethics from Homer onwards approved the notion that one's duty was to help the one group and harm the other: the poet Theognis (late sixth century BC) is expressing a perfectly traditional and acceptable sentiment when he asks for the great heaven to fall on him if he fails to help his *philoi* and bring pain and harm to his *echthroi* (869–72). Similarly, his younger contemporary, Solon, the Athenian statesman and law-giver, prays in a famous poem for prosperity and a good name 'and to be agreeable to friends and bitter to enemies, respected by the former and feared by the latter' (fr.13.5–6 West).

'Helping' was an all-inclusive idea: it might mean sharing between equals, or, for a socially superior or stronger *philos*, giving material benefits, protection and support in return for honour and service, while for a weaker *philos* the terms of the bargain were reversed, but in all cases what was envisaged was a reciprocal relationship. Thus in return for nurture and upbringing, parents could expect obedience from their children and support in their old age, and a rich and influential citizen could expect political backing from *philoi* who received his help. We might want to call this 'patronage', using a term derived from Roman society, but the relationship between *philoi* was perceived differently from that between Roman patrons and clients, which was by definition 'vertical' (Herman 1987: 38–9).

The notion of reciprocity applied to *echthroi* as well: the proper treatment for them was not neutrality or indifference, but actual harm, and in early Greece at any rate there was no embarrassment at public expression of the idea that one should pay back evil for evil and take pleasure in an enemy's troubles. A passage from Sophocles' *Antigone* illustrates these points well:

> *Creon*: Yes, son, you should have this resolve in your heart, to yield to your father's will in all things. It is for this that men pray to beget and bring up dutiful children, that they may pay back their father's enemy with evil and

> honour his *philos* as he would himself. But whoever
> begets useless children, what else would you say he
> does except beget troubles for himself and much
> laughter for his enemies? (639–47)

Creon is appealing here to well-established values and attitudes, though the traditional point of view did not go uncriticized: the action of the *Antigone* itself shows it up as too simple, and there is a famous critique in Book One of Plato's *Republic*.

There is another word for 'friend' which paradoxically enough can sometimes be used as the opposite of *philos*: the elusive word *xenos* (*xeinos* in some dialects), which means 'guest', 'host', 'stranger', 'foreigner' or even 'mercenary soldier', according to context. So *philoi* and *xenoi* can be opposed, in the same way as 'near' and 'far' or 'insiders' and 'outsiders'. Outsiders may be hostile or dangerous, but they can be linked to insiders by the special relationship of 'guest-friendship', *xenia*, a long-distance connection which depends just as much on reciprocal benefits and obligations as do *philos*-relationships.

Book Six of Homer's *Iliad* contains a memorable scene which illustrates attitudes to *xenia* and at the same time reminds us of the broader problem of identifying friends and enemies. Two major heroes prepare to meet in combat on the Trojan plain: the Achaean Diomedes and the Lycian Glaucus, who has come to fight on Priam's side. Diomedes does not know Glaucus and is impressed by the way he has been fighting. 'Who are you?' he asks, 'You are braver than the rest in facing my spear. If you are not a god in disguise come and fight me.' Glaucus begins by suggesting that since the generations of men come and go like leaves on the tree there is little point in asking him his lineage, but then he devotes sixty verses to a detailed account of his proud family history: he is grandson of the great Bellerophon, son of Glaucus, son of Sisyphus, son of Aeolus, a speech which delights Diomedes and causes him to put down his spear and greet Glaucus warmly:

> Why,
> you are my friend [*xeinos*]! My grandfather, Oeneus,
> made friends of us long years ago. He welcomed
> Prince Bellerophon to his great hall,
> his guest for twenty days. They gave each other
> beautiful tokens of amity: Grandfather's

13

offering was a loin-guard sewn in purple,
Bellerophon bestowed a cup of gold
two-handled: it is in my house, I left it there,
coming away to Troy. I cannot remember
Tydeus, my father – I was still too young
when he departed, when the Achaean army
came to grief at Thebes. I am your friend,
sworn friend [*xeinos philos*], in central Argos. You are mine
in Lycia, whenever I may come.
So let us keep from one another's
weapons in the spear-fights of this war.
Trojans a-plenty will be left for me,
and allies, as god puts them in my path;
many Achaeans will be left for you
to bring down if you can. Each take the other's
battle-gear: let those around us know
we have this bond of friendship from our fathers.

(Iliad 6.215–31 trans. Fitzgerald)

The reciprocity of the relationship is emphasized by the exchange of gifts between Oeneus and Bellerophon in the past and by the exchange of armour now proposed by Diomedes. The story ends with the wry comment that Glaucus was foolish enough to make an unequal exchange and let Diomedes give him bronze armour for gold. But there is no belittling of the *xenos*-relationship and its value.

There is some sense in our going back to early poetry, particularly Homer, for images and illustrations. It is true that the *Iliad* and the *Odyssey* were composed in the eighth century BC, before the city-state had properly come into being, and the world they evoke is a 'region of the mind', an ideal heroic past peopled by warrior chieftains and their followers rather than by citizens of the classical *polis*, but the poems evidently provided paradigms of action and experience which later centuries continued to find relevant. This must have been because there was some degree of continuity, at least in terms of perceptions, between archaic and later times. Gabriel Herman has recently made a persuasive case for the continuity of *xenia* as an institution with ancient roots. His argument runs on these lines:

When during the eighth and seventh centuries BC the contours of the city-state were gradually drawn, the ancient world was criss-crossed with an extensive network of personal alliances linking together all sorts of apolitical bodies (households, tribes, bands, etc.). The city framework superimposed itself upon this existing network – superimposed itself upon it, yet did not dissolve it. And when the city finally became established as the dominant form of organization, dense webs of guest-friendship still stretched beyond its bounds. Overtly or covertly, guest-friendship continued to act as a powerful bond between citizens of different cities and between citizens and members of various apolitical bodies. And by this persistence in the age of the cities, it became involved in actively shaping the value system of the *polis* and in formulating some of its most basic concepts and patterns of action.

(Herman 1987:6)

For our purposes the most important points stressed by Herman are the ritual structure of the relationship – the exchange of gifts and pledges which gave *xenia* an inalienable status comparable with that between *philoi* (*philia*) – and its likeness to *philia* in the reciprocity and reliance on trust. Its distinctiveness is to be seen in the physical separation of the participants and hence in the mainly upper-class character of *xenia* (the rich travelled more easily and more often) and in the far-reaching political implications of aristocratic networks which stretched beyond individual cities and even outside the Greek-speaking world.

As with *xenos*, the third Greek word for 'friend' has its paradigm case in the *Iliad*. Anyone looking for an example of a great friendship that has imprinted itself on Western literature can hardly overlook the relationship of Achilles and Patroclus. It is this relationship, and all that flows from it, particularly Achilles' grief and self-reproach over Patroclus' death and his subsequent rage against the Trojans, that dominate the latter half of the poem, and the word in question is *hetairos*, 'comrade'. This is the word ordinarily used at all periods for comrades-in-arms, companions, colleagues (sometimes interchangeably with *philos*), and it evidently could be associated with emotions of the deepest intensity and significance.

We might begin by noting what is given emphasis in the relationship between Achilles and Patroclus. Clearly there is something especially close about their comradeship: Patroclus is the only *hetairos* of Achilles mentioned by name in Book One (307, 337, 345); in Book Nine he alone is sitting with Achilles in his hut as Achilles plays his lyre (190–1), and he is the one who prepares the food and wine for Achilles' guests and makes the sacrifice before the meal (201–20); in Book Eleven it is he who is singled out by Nestor to talk to Achilles and try to prevail on him (765–97). What could have been emphasized instead was the fact that the two were blood relations – Patroclus' father Menoetius was half-brother of Aeacus, grandfather of Achilles – but this point is never explicitly made in the poem. When the early history of Achilles and Patroclus is recalled, all that is said is that Patroclus' father had brought him to the home of Achilles' father after an unfortunate accident in which the boy had killed a playmate (23.84–90; cf.11.765–90). The story of how Patroclus and Achilles were brought up together, with Patroclus, the elder, destined to be Achilles' *therapōn* ('squire') is told only in passing, and in general the close bond between the two is simply taken for granted.

There are two points worth noting here: first, the relationship is not one between strict equals, and yet it has the kind of ideal value for the two participants that in other cultures is associated with such friendships. Patroclus may be Achilles' *therapōn*, taking his orders and waiting on him, but he is irreplaceable in the eyes of Achilles, who says that having lost Patroclus he can suffer nothing worse, not even the loss of his father Peleus or of his only son Neoptolemus (19.319–37). All that matters after Patroclus' death is to punish the Trojans and give his dead *hetairos* due honour, and Achilles takes his revenge to such extremes, culminating in the dragging of the corpse of the defeated Hector around the walls of Troy, that the gods are constrained to intervene (Book Twenty-four). Thus the whole design of the plot depends on the special value attached by Achilles to his relationship with Patroclus, and its uniqueness is also more directly brought out in several remarkable passages. One of the most striking is Achilles' wish in Book Sixteen that everyone on both sides would be killed, apart from himself and Patroclus, so that the two alone might take Troy (97–100). In Book Twenty-three, when Patroclus' shade appears to the sleeping Achilles, asking for the burial of his corpse

16

and prophesying Achilles' own death, he has a further request to
make:

> One more message, one behest, I leave thee:
> not to inter my bones apart from thine
> but close together, as we grew together
> in thy family's hall. Menoetius
> from Opoeis had brought me, under a cloud,
> a boy still, on the day I killed the son
> of Lord Amphidamas – though I wished it not –
> in childish anger over a game of dice.
> Peleus, master of horse, adopted me
> and reared me kindly, naming me your squire.
> So may the same urn hide our bones, the one
> of gold your gracious mother gave.
>
> (82–92)

Achilles promises to do all he asks, and at the funeral he sees to it
that the bones of Patroclus are preserved in a golden urn until
such time as his own can be added (238–44). And on the pyre he
has sacrificed not only the customary horses and dogs but also
twelve Trojan youths – an outrage unique in the poem, identified
in the narrative as 'evil deeds' (23.176).

Equally telling is the lavish way in which Homer describes
Achilles' response to the news of Patroclus' death:

> A black storm-cloud of pain shrouded Achilles.
> On his bowed head he scattered dust and ash
> in handfuls and befouled his beautiful face,
> letting black ash sift on his fragrant chiton.
> Then in the dust he stretched his giant length
> and tore his hair with both hands. From the hut
> the women who had been spoils of war to him
> and to Patroclus flocked in haste around him,
> crying loud in grief. All beat their breasts,
> and trembling came upon their knees. Antilochus
> wept where he stood, bending to hold the hero's
> hands when groaning shook his heart: he feared
> the man might use sharp iron to slash his throat.
>
> (18.22–34)

The intensity of feeling evoked here leads to the second point: for a modern reader this might demand explanation in sexual terms, and indeed Greek readers in later times saw Achilles and Patroclus as archetypal lovers (Dover 1978: 196–7; Clarke 1978). Aeschylus wrote a tragic trilogy on the Iliadic story, and a small surviving fragment from one of the three plays (*Myrmidons*) speaks unequivocally of 'thighs' and 'kisses', while subsequent writers and scholars argued whether he was right to attribute an erotic relationship to Homer's heroes (Dover 1978: 196–201; Radt 1985: 250–1). In Aeschylus' time (first half of the fifth century BC) and for some generations before it Greek society had certainly valued homosexual attachments between men and boys, seeing them as (ideally) educational relationships in which the older man inspired the youth to emulate him as a soldier and a citizen, and in some cities these attitudes were accentuated by military organization which separated men from their families (Dover 1978: 191–4).

So what are we to make of Homer's silence? The *Iliad* and the *Odyssey* are not reticent about the fact of sexual activity as such, however circumspect they may be over the details (in Book Nine, for example, when Achilles causes Phoenix to stay overnight in his hut the sleeping arrangements are described: Patroclus saw to the making up of a bed for the old man, and then 'Achilles slept in the inner recess of the well-built hut, and with him lay a woman he had brought from Lesbos, Phorbas' daughter Diomede of the fair cheeks; on the other side of the hut lay Patroclus, and with him fair-girdled Iphis, whom Achilles gave him when he captured steep Scyros, city of Enyeus' (663–8; cf. Dover 1974: 207)). The poems may have suppressed features that did not seem to belong to the way of life of the vanished 'heroic age' that they were evoking; but it is even possible that for Homer the question of whether there was a sexual element in the relationship between Achilles and his 'dearest (most *philos*) *hetairos*' (17.411;19.315) was not the crucial one. Why Achilles should go to such extremes in his grief for Patroclus might be better explained in terms of the *Iliad*'s concern to explore human nature at the limits – the limits of anger, loss, violence, suffering, understanding – than in terms of a distinction between sexual and other kinds of intense feeling.

We should also remember that Achilles and Patroclus are no isolated example: the image of the pair of devoted comrades is a familiar one in the myths the Greeks told of their heroes, and one could cite Orestes and Pylades, Theseus and Pirithous, or Heracles and Iolaus as parallels. Their stories as originally told were not given a specifically homosexual interpretation, as Xenophon in his *Symposium* (8.31) makes Socrates point out. But in later times the Boeotians, who used homosexual relations as a principle of military organization, and whose 'Sacred Band' in the fourth century was an élite composed entirely of pairs of lovers, turned Heracles and Iolaus into such a pair, and the tomb of Iolaus at Thebes was treated as a sacred place for the exchange of lovers' pledges (Dover 1978: 199).

If we try to transpose the *hetairos*-relationship into the feminine gender, we immediately come up against the complex problem of interpreting the place of women in Greek society. Without entering that minefield, we might note that *hetaira*, the feminine of *hetairos*, is found much more commonly in the sense 'female sexual companion' (of a man) than 'female comrade' (of another woman; but cf. e.g. Lefkowitz and Fant 1982: 11). *Hetaira* in its commoner sense, traditionally translated 'courtesan', a word which has little meaning in modern English, could be used of anyone from a concubine to a high-class prostitute, though it is usually distinguishable from *pornē*, the word for the lowest grade of those who (as the Greeks put it) 'work with their bodies'. But friendship between women was undoubtedly important, as the evidence of literature and art makes plain. Nor is it surprising: in a society in which men's and women's pursuits were sharply differentiated, and respectable women were kept secluded from contact with men, particularly men who were not close *philoi*, there was a strong likelihood that women would spend much time, and form close ties, with one another. But such relationships are not given much detailed attention in literature: they usually occupy the background rather than the foreground (like the choruses in tragedy made up of *philai* sympathetic to one of the leading characters), and we get only rare glimpses of what a close relationship between women might mean.

The most famous of these is what survives of the lyric poetry of Sappho, which reflects the sophisticated society of Mytilene on Lesbos in the sixth century BC, a society seemingly less concerned than the Athens of Pericles to shut away its womenfolk. Sappho's poems evoke a world of aristocratic leisure in which cultivated women and girls share song, dance and religious activities and form intense emotional relationships. Scholars argue over the precise implications of these texts – the degree of physical intimacy, the nature of the cultic traditions involved – but for the student of ancient attitudes to friendship, one important fact stands out: erotic language could be used of ties that could also be identified as those of *philia*. (There is a parallel in what remains of Alcman's *Maiden Songs*; cf. e.g. Calame 1977; Burnett 1983.)

One way of looking at the whole question – a way, perhaps, of bringing out the difference between ancient and modern attitudes – is to note that while *philia* and the verb associated with it, *philein*, were inclusive terms, 'used in every context in which there were positive ties between people' (Finley 1977: 126), the noun *erōs* and the verb *erān* evoked specifically sexual love. From an ancient point of view the distinction could perhaps be most easily made in terms of presiding deities: the relationships between *philoi*, *xenoi* and *hetairoi* are characteristically watched over by Zeus, with help from Hestia and Hermes, while those between lovers are the sphere of Aphrodite and Eros. But a true lover would always be expected to *philein* as well as *erān* the beloved.

This brief survey of the main Greek words for 'friend', and of some dominant images of friendship in early Greek literature, may evoke for the modern reader a world very different from our own, interesting enough as an example of a sophisticated, pre-Christian culture which can offer contrasts with our own society, but not otherwise particularly relevant to a wider debate about friendship. But the picture needs to be supplemented with a few samples of what the Greeks had to offer by way of reflection on the subject. It soon becomes clear that, despite some apparent limitations – the ready-made nature of many *philoi*, for example – they had a highly-developed sense of the value of *philia* and of its potential as an ideal human relationship, and that their philosophers were interested in discussing it, in terms that have not been wholly superseded.

Plato's *Lysis*, the first surviving treatise on friendship from the Greek world, is a rather puzzling and elusive piece which seems designed to raise questions rather than provide answers, in the teasing and ironic manner characteristic of several of the early 'aporetic' dialogues. Two points in particular are worth noting. First, the setting of the dialogue is a wrestling school, where

Socrates meets the boy Lysis and his lover Hippothales, along with Lysis' friend Menexenus and *his* lover Ctesippus; although the subject he ultimately discusses with the boys is friendship and not sexual love, it is no part of the purpose of the dialogue to draw a sharp distinction between the two (cf. Friedländer 1965: 102–4). Secondly, teasing as the dialogue is (it plays first with the idea that friendship depends on the appeal of like to like, then with the notion that it is a relationship of opposites), it asks important questions about reciprocity and about the possibility that friendship is a means by which imperfect human beings can learn goodness.

This moral emphasis is strongly reinforced by Aristotle in his more systematic treatment of the subject in Books Eight and Nine of the *Nicomachean Ethics*. For Aristotle, who classifies friendship under three headings, according to whether its object is utility, pleasure or goodness, the best kind of friendship is between 'people who are good, alike in virtue' (1156b7). He discusses reciprocity, considering examples of unequal friendship, such as that between parents and children, and compares reciprocity in friendship with that involved in other sorts of community, e.g. the relations between fellow citizens. He also deals with the principles on which friendship should be practised, with its basis in a particular kind of self-love, and with the necessity of friendship for happiness. As in Plato, there is no attempt to restrict friendship to associations between say, non-lovers or non-kin: the philosophers have no difficulty in working within the traditional definition of *philia*, but they insist on moral distinctions within the socially defined categories.

A couple of samples will illustrate the serious attention paid by Aristotle to what he sees as a crucial element in the happiness of the good man. Book Eight of the *Nicomachean Ethics* justifies the inclusion of a discussion of friendship on the grounds that friendship is a virtue, or implies virtue,

> and is besides most necessary with a view to living. For without friends no one would choose to live, though he had all other goods; even rich men and those in possession of office and of dominating power are thought to need friends most of all; for what is the use of prosperity without the opportunity of beneficence, which is exercised chiefly and in its most

laudable form towards friends? Or how can prosperity be guarded and preserved without friends? The greater it is, the more exposed it is to risk. And in poverty and in other misfortunes men think friends are the only refuge. It helps the young, too, to keep from error; it aids older people by ministering to their needs and supplementing the activities that are failing from weakness; those in the prime of life it stimulates to noble actions – 'two going together' [*Iliad* 10.224] – for with friends men are more able both to think and to act. Again, parent seems by nature to feel it for offspring and offspring for parent, not only among men but among birds and among most animals; it is felt mutually by members of the same race, and especially by men, when we praise lovers of their fellowmen. We may even see in our travels how near and dear every man is to every other. Friendship seems too to hold states together, and lawgivers to care more for it than for justice; for unanimity seems to be something like friendship, and this they aim at most of all, and expel faction as their worst enemy; and when men are friends they have no need of justice, while when they are just they need friendship as well, and the truest form of justice is thought to be a friendly quality.

(1155a 4–32, trans. Ross)

The indispensability of friends is brought out again in a well-known passage at the end of Book Nine:

It is also disputed whether the happy man will need friends or not. It is said that those who are supremely happy and self-sufficient have no need of friends ... But it seems strange, when one assigns all good things to the happy man, not to assign friends, who are thought the greatest of external goods. And if it is more characteristic of a friend to do well by another than to be well done by, and to confer benefits is characteristic of the good man and of virtue, and it is nobler to do well by friends than by strangers, the good man will need people to do well by. This is why the question is asked whether we need friends more in prosperity or in adversity, on the assumption that not only does a man in adversity need people to confer benefits on him, but also those who are prospering need people to do well by. Surely it is strange, too,

22

to make the supremely happy man a solitary; for no one would choose the whole world on condition of being alone, since man is a political creature and one whose nature is to live with others. Therefore even the happy man lives with others; for he has the things that are by nature good. And plainly it is better to spend his days with friends and good men than with strangers or any chance persons. Therefore the happy man needs friends.

(1169b 3–22; trans. Ross)

These attitudes were certainly not confined to the philosophers or originated by them: both Plato and Aristotle quote proverbial sayings about *philia* which suggest the high value traditionally set on it by their society. It is no accident that this is often defined in terms of material goods, the everyday language of evaluation: 'There is nothing better than a true *philos*, not wealth, not royal power. And the exchange value of a true *philos* is not to be calculated' (Euripides, *Orestes* 1155–7; cf. Sophocles, *Philoctetes* 671–3. The poets seem to be echoing a popular formulation). Another familiar idea was that friends shared everything: 'the things of *philoi* are in common', a proverb often quoted (e.g. by Euripides, *Orestes* 735). *Philos*-relationships were ideally characterized by sharing, openness, trust, absence of the profit motive. Of course, if bad people were friends they could use their *philia* for bad ends – nepotism, political faction, sensual indulgence, corruption – hence the concern of Aristotle to distinguish between the objects of friendship in terms of utility, pleasure and goodness.

These widely shared ideas about *philia* are neatly illustrated by a passage in Xenophon's *Hieron*, a short work on the problems of autocratic rule, which takes the form of an imaginary dialogue between Hieron, tyrant of Syracuse in the early fifth century, and the poet Simonides, one of his most famous protégés. Hieron's point is that the tyrant's lot is deeply unsatisfactory, because there is no one he can trust. *Philia* is a great good for human beings: the person who has *philoi* is always welcome to his friends, and they take pleasure in doing good to him, they miss him if he's absent, are delighted when he returns, rejoice in his success, and help him in his difficulties. But tyrants have a smaller share in this valuable possession, *philia*, than anyone else.

Think about it this way, Simonides, if you want to see the
truth of what I say. Obviously the firmest ties of *philia* are
between parents and children, between siblings, between
wives and husbands and between *hetairoi*. . . .Now you will find
that private persons are indeed most loved by people in these
categories, but when it comes to tyrants, many have killed
their own children or been killed by them, many brothers
have murdered one another, many have been destroyed by
their own wives and by *hetairoi* who seemed to be their dearest
philoi. So when people are actually hated by those most likely,
either by natural disposition or through social or moral
obligation, to love them, how can we suppose that anyone else
will be their *philoi*?

(Chapter 3)

Throughout antiquity, friendship continued to be a topic for
serious ethical debate, though most of the treatises that dealt with
it have been lost. This long tradition of Greek discourse lies behind
the most famous work on friendship to have survived from
Classical times, Cicero's *De Amicitia*, which frequently refers – not
always without polemic – to the Greek philosophers, even though
its main concern is with Republican Roman society and the values
and perceptions of the Roman governing class. In Cicero's
dialogue, composed in 44 BC (the year of Caesar's murder) for his
own friend Atticus, the paradigm case is not a heroic partnership
like that of Achilles and Patroclus but the famous friendship
between Scipio Africanus the younger and Gaius Laelius, who were
statesmen and soldiers, as well as influential patrons of literature
and philosophy, in Rome in the second century BC.

However much he may differ from the Greek writers in method
and style, Cicero shares their fundamental belief that without
friendship, life does not make sense. The dialogue ends with
Laelius' words about what his relationship with Scipio has meant
to him:

For myself, of all the blessings given me by fortune or nature
there is nothing I could compare with the friendship of
Scipio. In this friendship I found agreement on political
issues, advice on private business, and the most delightful way
of enjoying my leisure. I never offended him in even the most
trivial matter, at least not so far as I was aware, and I never

24

heard him say anything I would not have wished to hear. We had one home between us; we kept the same style of life and shared our meals, not only on our military campaigns but also on our foreign tours and country vacations. I need not mention our constant devotion to learning and research, in which we spent all our leisure time secluded from the public. If my capacity to recollect and remember all this had died along with Scipio I should have no means of bearing the loss of one so near and dear to me. But the experiences I shared with him are not dead; in fact they are strengthened and made more vivid by reflection and memory. . . .

(27.103–4)

Cicero's world is a far cry from Homer's, and his discussion of friendship is grounded in a discussion of virtue along philosophical lines, but the intensity of personal feeling attached to the relationship is something that has its model in early Greek poetry.

REFERENCES

Burnett, A. P. (1983) *Three Archaic Poets: Archilochus, Alcaeus, Sappho*, London: Duckworth.

Calame, C. (1977) *Les choeurs de jeunes filles en Grèce archaïque*, 2 vols, Rome: ed. Ateneo e Bizzarri.

Clarke, W. M. (1978) 'Achilles and Patroclus in love', *Hermes* 106: 381–96.

Dover, K. J. (1978) *Greek Homosexuality*, London: Duckworth.

——(1974) *Greek Popular Morality*, Oxford: Basil Blackwell.

Finley, M. I. (1977) *The World of Odysseus*, 2nd ed. London: Penguin.

Fitzgerald, R. (1984) *Homer, the Iliad*, Oxford: Oxford University Press.

Friedländer, P. (1965) trans. H. Meyerhoff, *Plato II, The Dialogues, First Period*, London: Routledge & Kegan Paul.

Herman, G. (1987) *Ritualised Friendship and the Greek City*, Cambridge: Cambridge University Press.

Hooker, J. T. (1987) 'Homeric φιλοζ', *Glotta* 65: 44–65.

Lefkowitz, M. and Fant, M. (1982) *Women's Life in Greece and Rome*, London: Duckworth.

Radt, S. (1985) *Tragicorum Graecorum Fragmenta*, vol. 3: *Aeschylus*, Göttingen: Vandenhoeck und Rupprecht.

Ross, W. D. (1925) *The Works of Aristotle translated into English*, vol. IX, Oxford: Oxford University Press.

Chapter Two

FRIENDSHIP IN THE CHRISTIAN TRADITION

GILLIAN AND STEPHEN R. L. CLARK

CLASSICAL IDEALS AND OTHERS

Greater love hath no man than this, that he lay down his life for his friends

(John 15:13)

This saying of Jesus means something to people for whom 'John 15:13' means nothing. It is engraved on war memorials and used in praise of those who died to help the victims of disaster. Self-sacrifice is not an exclusively Christian virtue, but Christians say that the life and death and continuing inspiration of Jesus Christ have transformed human possibilities and human relationships: we need not limit our concern to ourselves and the few people who naturally matter in our lives. Jesus prefaced his saying on friendship with 'This is my command, that you love one another as I have loved you'. What then is the Christian tradition of friendship, and who are the friends for whom we should, if necessary, be ready to die? People we know and love? People who share beliefs, or culture, or just humanity with us? People who just happen to be there, like the victims of war and disaster?

Christian tradition is not formed in isolation from the general culture. What Christians have had to say about friendship depends on what they think it is, and that has varied greatly. Christianity took shape, and the New Testament was written, in the Graeco-Roman world described by Professor Easterling. There the obligations of friendship were taken very seriously, not least because the state did not provide social services. To reverse Jeremy Taylor's aphorism (see Meilaender (1981): 25ff.): 'when charity was little, friendships were the noblest things in the world'. Friendship was much more extensive than the freely-chosen, affective relationship we now call friendship, though such friendships were known and enjoyed. Friends were the people with whom you were connected: the Greek word *philos*, commonly translated 'friend', means 'one who belongs to you'. The connection might be by blood or marriage or country, shared political beliefs or philosophy of life or personal pleasures, favours given and received; it might or might not include warm feelings; it certainly involved a commitment. Friends were essential to mere survival and to worldly success: the vocabulary of friendship, kinship, love, and patronage overlapped just as the relationships did.

Aristotle produced a classification of friendships (in *Nicomachean Ethics* 8 and 9) which many Christian writers have found helpful: friendships are based on pleasure, utility, or shared concern for what is truly good. The third kind was the highest, and the classic examples of friendship (still known to fans of the classically-educated P. G. Wodehouse) were Damon and Pythias. They were members of a Pythagorean community in Sicily, which aimed to transcend private interest and unite many people in the pursuit of truth and goodness. The local tyrant had Pythias condemned to death, and granted him time to settle his affairs only on condition that someone stood hostage. To the tyrant's double amazement, Damon volunteered and Pythias returned in time (Iamblichus, *On the Pythagorean Life*: 234–6). That was real friendship: disinterested, committed, and founded on the common love of goodness.

> True friendship, indeed,
> of nought but of virtue doth truly proceed
> (Richard Edwards, *Damon and Pithias* 127 ff.)

When Ambrose of Milan discussed Christian friendship, in the fourth century AD, he was well within the Classical tradition, and indeed borrowed wholesale from Cicero. Ambrose, a high-ranking civil servant who had become bishop unexpectedly, was a celibate writing for a (mostly) celibate male clergy. The church accepted the possibility of friendship between men and women who were not related by blood or by marriage, but shared the classical suspicion that such friendships would not remain asexual. Christian women living as celibates at home or in all-female communities (a Christian departure from classical tradition) were carefully guarded from scandal. Marriages were arranged by families, a husband might be much older than his wife and was almost certain to have much more education and experience, and the majority Christian view (at least among those who wrote about it) was that marriage was, for both sexes, a second-best to celibacy, a remedy for the fallen state of humanity. So Ambrose discusses friendship partly in terms of ranking one's obligations (mostly financial) to kin, church members, claimants on charity; partly as the best human relationship, which allows good men to encourage each other in the service of God.

> Preserve, then, my sons, the friendship you have entered into
> with your brethren. Nothing is lovelier in the world of men. It
> is indeed a consolation in this life to have someone to whom
> to open your heart, with whom you can share your secrets, to
> whom you can commit the privacy of your mind, a
> consolation to choose for yourself a faithful man to
> congratulate you when things go well, sympathize in your
> sadness, encourage you under opposition.
>
> (Ambrose, *De Officiis Ministrorum* 3: 22)

Aelred of Rievaulx, writing for a monastic community in the twelfth century, followed Cicero and Ambrose in his praise of friendship. Perhaps one should hesitate to say that 'God is friendship' (as the phrase lacks canonical authority), but that 'most gracious love, happy embracing, blissful charity whereby the Father rests in the Son and the Son in the Father' is the life to which true friends may grow:

> And so a friend cleaving to his friend in the spirit of Christ
> becomes one heart and soul with him and thus, rising by the
> steps of love to the friendship of Christ, is made one spirit
> with him in one [spiritual] kiss.
>
> (Squire 1969: 41, 106)

At the opposite pole is an equally committed Christian, C. S. Lewis. *The Four Loves* (1963) was apparently written from the perspective of a bachelor don, celibate and of the educated élite like Ambrose, sharing in a college life which had some affinities with monasticism, but in a culture which took marriage as the central human relationship. He envisages a world of couples, the husband having same-sex friends at work and for relaxation, the wife (he supposes) having same-sex friends at home; it is a mistake to try and combine these relationships. Lewis's friends spoke with some feeling about his indifference to their wives. In his indifference to them he was also indifferent to those aspects of his thinking-companions' lives. It is difficult for us to understand how he could have written with such distaste for the 'intellectual pretensions' of women when he had been married for four years before the book was first published, and had spent all his working life in universities with women's colleges. How exactly did Joy Davidman, his wife, react to his claim (1963: 72) that it is 'only the riff-raff of either sex that wants to be incessantly hanging on the other', i.e. enjoys real and intellectual friendships with people of the other sex?

'Friends' are united, on Lewis's account, by their shared devotion to ideas and ideals, not by their being 'one heart, one soul', in the sense that runs back through Aelred and Augustine all the way to Aristotle. And it is apparently axiomatic that men and women must have widely different ideas and ideals: so widely different, indeed, that Lewis can hardly believe that women even have 'friends', in Lewis's sense, of their own sex. Some feminist writers, unable to believe that men and boys might, being human, have close friendships of their own, now try to reverse this claim. So friendship, one of the Four Loves, is for Lewis a kind of luxury, not necessary for survival or for virtue, but giving value to survival, like those other luxuries, art and philosophy. It has no biological imperative, like sexual desire and parental love. We might set beside this a remark of St Augustine, that God, in creating woman, obviously had reproduction in mind: for any other purpose, like companionship or combined effort, another man would have been much more useful (*De Genesi ad litteram*, 9: 5).

Somewhere in between Ambrose and Lewis, as far as families and friends are concerned, is Jane Austen, a clergyman's daughter, reserved but deeply Christian in the manner of the early nineteenth century. *Mansfield Park*, she said, had ordination as its subject, but like all her books it is much concerned with friendship. It conveys the same message as popular preachers of the time, who made good use of Aristotle's classification (Dwyer 1987). Friendships for pleasure are shallow if not dangerous; friendships for advancement are suspect; disinterested friendship is an essential training in goodness, self-control and sensitivity to the needs of others, and is most likely to be found within the immediate family circle: parents and children, brothers and sisters, husband and wife. The gulf in experience between men (who leave home for school and university, and travel, and enter professions or trades) and women (who are educated at home and will remain there if they do not marry) seems not to affect their moral and religious awareness, and that is what counts.

These examples are enough to show how friendship has been differently interpreted and differently placed in the hierarchy of values. Recent writers, at least in the industrial West, have been more inclined to emphasize emotional than financial need, and to equate training in goodness with the expression of love: friendship for individuals can lead you to a wider love for humankind (an argument derived, mistakenly, from Plato and used by Augustine: Meilaender 1981: 16–24), and friendship has a peculiar value in that friends do not have to like you or put up with you, but love you for what you are. Some accounts of the I-Thou relationship, or the encounter with the Other, show an intense awareness of human contact but seem a long way removed from ordinary dealings with the friends who drop in for coffee or whom you haven't seen for years. This perhaps gives the impression that friendship is a neglected topic; and it is true that you are unlikely to find an entry under 'Friendship' in dictionaries of Christian thought or Christian ethics. But consultation of the entry under 'Love' will show that Christian thinking about friendship is part of a wider preoccupation with proper human – and creaturely – relationships. This concern is as intense as ever; and, despite the variations, some problems keep recurring.

THE HOUSEHOLD OF FAITH

Here are my mother and my brothers: whoever does the will of my heavenly father is my brother, my sister, my mother

(Matthew 12: 50)

Jesus said this of his followers, when he was interrupted in his teaching with the news that his mother and brothers were waiting to see him. Some sects have thought that he thereby rejected the natural family, but the general Christian view is that he extended the family bond, the commitment we take for granted, to all who serve God. Christians have always liked family terms: 'father' for priest or abbot, 'mother' for senior nun and now also for priest, 'brother' and 'sister' for fellow-Christians, especially for those who have replaced their natural families by a family based on shared religious commitment, that is a religious order. The family language is meant to express the closeness of the bond: as we would say of a close friend or a companion animal, 'she's one of the family.' Friends are those with whom we are 'at home'. The Society of Friends preserves, in its title, an early Christian usage of calling a group of Christians 'the friends' or perhaps 'the family', 'the dear ones': again, it depends on the translation of the Greek *philos* in 3 John 15 and perhaps Acts 27: 3, and it may well be relevant that the New Testament discusses household relationships but not friendships.

But how do the claims of the natural family rank in relation to those of the Christian 'family of friends'? Married clergy nowadays have Ambrose's problem of allocating money combined with the even more insoluble problem of allocating time. 'There are as many different kinds of claim upon our neighbourly charity as there are different kinds of relationship' (Squire 1969: 46 after Aelred). There is a strong Christian tradition of renouncing close personal ties in order to devote oneself to prayer and service, but celibates in pastoral work, without the support of a religious community, have equal problems with loneliness. They do not want to put off their parishioners by having 'favourites', but they do need friends: many Christians would say it is of great importance to recognize that we are emotionally needy, not self-sufficient, that hardly any of us can manage without the love of our fellow-beings conveying to us the love of God. In the Genesis narrative, God made humanity double, not single, because it is not good for human beings to be alone. And the tradition of self-renouncing love, which makes no claims of its own and exercises no power, becomes disquieting when seen from the receiving end. Would it be possible to make a relationship with someone who really wants nothing from you, not even a return of love and concern? 'I don't want charity!' is a protest which makes the point. Charity is *caritas*, the Latin word for 'dearness' which most nearly translates Greek *philia*. Something has gone wrong when charity is experienced as a way of keeping human relationships at arm's length.

31

Again, how do the claims of the Christian family relate to those who are simply in need? Jesus taught that in giving clothes or food or water to the 'least of my brothers', we give to him (Matthew 25: 40 and 45): but did he mean by that the children of God, all those whom God has created and loves, or the unassuming servants of God, the followers of Jesus? Just as the original Levitical commandment (Leviticus 19:18) to 'love one's neighbour' refers primarily to one's fellow Israelite, and to others only by extension, the love required of 'adoptive Israelites' may not be, first of all, for 'just any other human being', but for other members of the spiritual Israel. One of us remembers hearing a strong case for this second interpretation at a New Testament conference. 'That's all very well,' said a voice at the back, 'but what's my text in Christian Aid Week?'

When people are in immediate need of food and clothes and water, and Christian Aid and other relief agencies swing into action, they do not discriminate according to the religious and political and moral standing of those in danger of death. Christian Aid, as its collectors often have to explain, is not restricted to Christian donors and recipients. But is that the right response to all needs? Should we assume that, because Christ died for all people, all people should be counted as part of the household of faith? Pagan philosophers often spoke of themselves as 'citizens of the world' and emphasized the bonds of actual or potential friendship that united folk of many races. Later commentators have seen universal humanism in such remarks, as though the sages were advocating an undiscriminating love of human beings everywhere. But the sages themselves were speaking of the friendship of 'the wise', and expressly denied that good and wicked people could be 'friends' (Clark 1987). Christians have agreed: 'even the most perverse have to be loved [sc. we should wish them well, and pray for their redemption], but it is clear that there cannot be any community of will and opinion between the good and evil' (Squire 1969: 105, after Aelred). Indeed it is doubtful that there could be such a community of will and opinion between the good and those who, without being evil, are ordinarily foolish and self-willed. But those Christians who lay great stress on the redemptive grace of God, and see little or no value in human goodness, might not think there is that much difference among people: we are all sinners, we cannot discriminate.

NEIGHBOUR-LOVE

If you love only those who love you, what reward can you expect? Even the tax-collectors do that much

(Matthew 5: 46)

So ordinary pagans may find their friends among their family, their class-mates, their fellow-hobbyists and thinking-companions. The wise are not misled by outward seeming, and find friends wherever truth and justice are honoured. Both sorts of friendship are matters of preferring some people to others. Some commentators see a contradiction here. In Johnson's words (discussed by Meilaender 1981: 7ff.):

All friendship is preferring the interest of a friend, to the neglect, or perhaps, against the interest of others; so that an old Greek said, 'He that has friends, has no friend'. Now Christianity recommends universal benevolence, to consider all men as our brethren; which is contrary to the virtue of friendship, as described by the ancient philosophers.

(Boswell 1953: 945ff.)

It is one of the few occasions when Johnson actually conceded defeat in an argument: his opponent, Mrs Knowles, pointed out that 'the household of faith' had, on occasion, preference, and that Jesus himself had one disciple whom especially he loved. But the dispute continues.

Christians are expected to extend help and concern beyond the Christian group, to 'love your enemies'. 'Enemies' is perhaps an over-translation: the word does not mean someone who sets out to destroy you, but someone not your friend, who may be expected to advance the interests of himself and his against those of you and yours. 'Look after your competitors' might make the point for the 1980s. But if Christians are not allowed to do down the opposition, or at least not to leave it in distress, are they allowed to have friends? William Blake posed the problem bluntly:

He who loves his Enemies betrays his Friends;
This surely is not what Jesus intends

(Blake 1966: 751)

But what did Jesus intend? May Christians have 'preferred people', whom they like, with whom they feel at ease, whom they are ready to help? Some theologians (of whom Kierkegaard is the most widely known) have argued as Johnson did that 'preferential relationships', based on liking and shared interests, fall short of properly Christian love for all God's people; they may even be an expression of self-love, of indulgence of our feelings. We ought instead to show active friendship to all whom we encounter in life, 'neighbour-love'.

That, after all, is the moral of the Good Samaritan story, which Jesus told when a lawyer to whom he was talking wanted to know (as many later Christians have done) who exactly counts as the neighbour we have to love (Luke 10: 29–37). The Samaritan did not live next door to the victim of muggers, freedom-fighters or terrorists, whom he found on the road to Jericho. He belonged to a different religious and political grouping; he had never seen the man before, and for all he knew the victim might be a mugger, or a terrorist, himself. Nevertheless, he was 'neighbour' to the man, going to some trouble and expense to help him recover. Moral theologians influenced by this tradition sometimes gravely exaggerate (or, to other eyes, impugn) the Samaritan's 'virtue' as being a 'love not fitted for society', as though he had immediately abandoned all other, normal claims upon his time and money.

This 'neighbour-love' of those you meet, unqualified by personal ties or indeed by merit, is often called by the Greek name *agape*, in the hope of marking a distinctively Christian kind of relationship: as such it is often opposed to the personal tie of friendship, which is given the Greek name *philia*. Classically-trained theologians point out, at intervals, that *agape* in the New Testament and contemporary texts does not have a distinctively Christian use: it overlaps with *philia*, which (as usual) means any relationship of 'belonging' (Moffatt 1929; Furnish 1972). Nor is there a clear opposition between *agape* and *erōs*, love which seeks the good of the beloved and love which seeks the beloved for itself, as Anders Nygren argued (Nygren 1932). *Erōs*, now used specifically of sexual love, is used in Greek philosophical tradition of the soul's desire for God, just as Christian mystics have used the metaphor of physical passion and union. The Greek translation of the Hebrew scriptures, the *Septuagint*, uses *agape* to translate the Hebrew *ahebh* even where it seems, from Nygren's perspective, clearly equivalent to *erōs* (Burnaby 1967). This is not just a point of historical interest. Varieties of loving and liking overlap, as the words which describe them do: we are used, these days, to recognizing a sexual undercurrent in friendship or in parental love (for which theologians like to use yet another Greek term, *storge*, though Greeks used it also for sexual love). It is difficult or impossible to do a taxonomy of love, separating out four (or more) loves and labelling one of them Christian.

Some saints, perhaps, achieve undifferentiated love for all they meet, and are so close to God that they do not need human comfort. Ordinary Christians are not like that, and most see no need to abandon their normal range of likings, unless these tend to corrupt. Even Jesus, as Mrs Knowles observed, had special friends: Lazarus, 'the disciple whom Jesus loved', the inner circle with whom he would withdraw from the crowds. And what is the content of 'love' in 'love your neighbour'? John Burnaby (1967) says the command does not simply mean 'help your neighbour in distress', any more that the prior command to love God means 'do God's will' (see Outka 1972: 93). But what the Samaritan actually did was to help his neighbour in distress, and we know nothing of his feelings except that he showed compassion. As ordinary Christians are given to remarking, you have to love your fellow-Christians, but nobody said you had to like them. Nor do most Christians find it possible to make an emotional commitment to more than a few people. Anyone who has tried seriously to pray through the intercessions knows how difficult it is to switch from the bishop to the local church whose turn it is, to the church overseas whose turn it is, to the latest victims of war or emergency, to the list of parishioners in distress. We do not have endless resources even of prayer and benevolence, let alone of active love and, especially, of time. The Samaritan himself, even if he was as exaggeratedly dedicated to the man he helped as Meilaender supposes (1981: 34), did not spend his life wandering the byways of Palestine to discover victims, nor did he organize an international 'Victims Aid'.

All men are to be loved equally. But since you cannot do good to all, you are to pay special regard to those who, by the accidents of time, or place, or circumstance, are brought into closer connection with you . . . as by a sort of lottery

    (Augustine, *On Christian Doctrine* 1: 28; Meilaender 1981: 19)

There is good reason to argue that (as Aristotle said: *Politics* 1: 1253a1ff.) the tendency to form groups and relationships is just as 'biological', just as much part of the human blueprint, as pair-bonding in marriage. It would still be possible to say, as Ambrose's Christians did about marriage, that friendship belongs to a fallen world, and that Christians can rise above it; but most Christians have sided rather with Joseph Butler, the eighteenth-century philosopher and preacher who founded an ethic on the natural human delight in connections. Even those who praise 'universal charity' as 'the special characteristic of Christian love' will often add that 'it would be sinful and may even be gravely sinful to overturn the order in essential matters, e.g. to give preference to one's more distant relatives to the neglect of one's spouse, children or parents' (Peschke 1978: II, 186). Provided we do not become over-partial, and blinded to the needs of those outside our circle, friendship is a force for good: and, as Butler pointed out, there is a fallacy in claiming that friendship only gratifies my self-love, for it would not be gratifying unless I already cared for my friend. Christians like Aelred have gone further: the best kind of friendship, a reciprocal, disinterested delight in what one's friend is, may be an image of God's love for us and ours for God.

GOD AS FRIEND

You are my friends, if you do what I command you. I no longer call you servants, for the servant does not know what his master is doing: I called you friends, because I have made known to you all that I have heard from my father

(John 15: 14–15)

How is it possible to be a friend of God? Aristotle suspected that the disparity between mortal and immortal was simply too great (*Nicomachean Ethics* 8: 1158b35ff.). The author of another text in the Aristotelian corpus, the *Magna Moralia*, thought it would be sheerly ridiculous to claim to be God's friend (*Magna Moralia* 2: 1208b30ff.). But classical tradition did not reject the idea of mortals being dear to the gods (*theophiles*), and some philosophers held that the wise were indeed friends of God, rising to some understanding of the divine mind. Christians were often accused of lacking or despising wisdom, preaching to simple people a revelation which had been conveyed without any preference for the wise. 'Hath not God made foolish the wisdom of this world?' (Paul, I Corinthians 1: 20). Ambrose, though in other contexts he could link Christianity with the philosophical understanding of God, offers his clergy a quite simple exposition of John 15. God has shared his thoughts with us; we can share our thoughts with him, and carry out his wishes. This is a relationship of confidence, as reciprocal as a finite human being can decently expect, and offered to all who love God. But theologians who insist on a radical contrast between Christian *agape* and any natural love also reject the possibility of a relationship with God which resembles human love or friendship. Thus Nygren claims that one should not expect to 'love' or be 'friends with' God, but rather to have 'faith' in Him (1932: I, 66). This requires him to reject John's Gospel as only dubiously Christian, and strangely endorses Aristotle's judgement.

Many Christians would disagree. Evangelical piety of the late eighteenth and nineteenth centuries encouraged a sense of strong personal relationship with Jesus, and the hymns of this period are still much loved. 'What a friend we have in Jesus', 'my Saviour and my Friend', 'there's a friend for little children above the bright blue sky': friendship here is envisaged as guidance and support, like the moral friendships in school stories of the time. Some theologians find this relationship altogether too cosy, and would like to recall Aristotle's sense of the immense distance between God and human, but their congregations include many who say they experience the close bond revealed in Jesus' earthly existence. But this strongly personal model of being friends with God is not the only possibility. One of the most interesting recent discussions, by Sallie McFague, moves the emphasis away from the reciprocal one-to-one relationship to the possibility of being friends with many people, and indeed with non-humans (1987: 157ff.). Thinking-companions, *pace* Lewis, are not our only friends. Saints are those who find their friends outside the normal boundaries of class, race, creed – or even species (on which see James Serpell, later in this volume, and Clark 1983). This 'ecological' model of friendship uses one of the most ancient and valued Christian symbols, the shared meal, which Jesus made an expression of friendship not only within the Christian group, but also with those who had exploited their fellow-creatures but could

learn a better way, like tax-collectors and sinners (Luke 5:30).
Another non-Jew, a Canaanite woman this time, brought out an
implication of the shared meal.

> 'It is not right to take the children's bread
> and throw it to the dogs.'
> 'True, Lord, but the dogs eat the scraps
> that fall from the masters' table.'
>
> (Matthew 15: 26–7)

Once again, the teaching is not to neglect our natural obligations,
but to recognize that there is enough for others too. And, once
again, there is an ancient tradition, reinterpreted by Christian
thinkers, of understanding friendship as that which unites the
universe.

Aelred saw the reciprocal love of Father and Son, united in the
Holy Spirit, as a model of friendship, and the still centre of the
turning world. 'Every single thing, from the highest angel to the
smallest worm, has about it some reminiscence of the divine
charity which is as intimate to it as charity is to the life of God'
(Squire 1969: 41). And the exchange of love goes beyond
reciprocity. The Trinity is three persons, each of whom exchanges
love with two others, and rejoices in the interchange of the other
two. Renaissance philosophers and theologians borrowed an
image from pagan tradition, the ball-game. The ball-player, as
Chrysippus observed, has mastered the art of giving and receiving,
and the dance goes on as long as the balls are kept up in the air
(Seneca, *De Beneficiis* 2: 17: 3).

> The golden apple of selfhood, thrown among the false gods,
> became an apple of discord because they scrambled for it.
> They did not know the first rule of the holy game, which is
> that every player must by all means touch the ball and then
> immediately pass it on.
>
> (Lewis 1957: 141; see Meilaender 1981: 51ff.)

Pagan and Christian tradition agree that the dance or game or
exchange of love is spoilt when we insist on having things 'our
way', and holding on to what we think is ours: our belongings, our
purposes, our satisfaction. Self-will, *authadeia*, is the cause of the
soul's fall (Plotinus, *Enneads* 4: 8: 4ff.). If instead we reckon the
good of our friends as our own good, we find that everything is

ours (as, of course, it is everyone else's). Stoic philosophers constructed a syllogism to set out the argument. The wise are friends of God, in that they love God not only by nature, but in full awareness. Friends have everything in common. Everything belongs to God; so everything belongs to the wise. There are at least two significant elements in this doctrine. Firstly, that the wise (and correspondingly, those united with Christ Jesus) are not subject to the laws of nations, even if they do not generally break them.

> Dare any of you, having a matter against another, go to law
> before the unjust, and not before the saints? Do you not know
> that the saints shall judge the world. . .? Know ye not that we
> shall judge angels? How much more things that pertain to this
> life?
>
> (Paul, I Corinthians 6: 1ff.)

Secondly, that the true possessor of any natural good is not its proprietor, but she who rightly and worshipfully enjoys it.

> You never enjoy the world aright, till the Sea itself floweth in
> your veins, till you are clothed with the heavens, and crowned
> with the stars: and perceive yourself to be the sole heir of the
> whole world, and more than so, because men are in it who are
> every one sole heirs as well as you . . . Yet further, you never
> enjoy the world aright, till you so love the beauty of enjoying
> it, that you are covetous and earnest to persuade others to
> enjoy it.
>
> (Traherne 1960: 14–15)

Friendship with God, then, may become a model for ready acceptance of needs and claims, for willingness to let go of what we thought was ours, in return for a share in all there is. We are back at the question with which we began: does this mean abandoning all claims of our own, or of our own friends and dear ones? Not all Christians have thought this: inordinate or greedy self-love does not bring all 'self-love' into disrepute.

> That a man should love his own happiness is as necessary to
> his nature as the faculty of the will is; and it is impossible that
> such a love should be destroyed in any other way than by
> destroying his being.
>
> (Edwards 1969: 159)

To love others is to make their happiness essential to one's own, and if one did not desire that latter how could one desire theirs? Conversely, 'God is Love, and you are His object. . . He is happy in you when you are happy: as parents in their children' (Traherne 1960: 24).

Yet some Christians have seen an obligation for us to renounce all our own claims, to attend only to the needs of others, laying down our lives in life as well as death. Niebuhr's account of *agape* (on which see Vaughan 1983: 38ff.) takes self-abnegation to its apparent limit. Sacrificial or divine love is an utter heedlessness to the interests or the self-chosen policies of the self. As such it must always be powerless, a deliberate refusal to exert any power over others or the world itself, a refusal even to bid for one result rather than another. Friendship comes off badly by comparison: it is merely mutual love, a second best. We are to love God by doing whatever we are required to do by whomever it is we happen to encounter, without any regard for consequences or our own wills. Unsurprisingly, such a vocation is rarely fulfilled, and Niebuhr's 'praise' of it amounts, in practice, to the recommendation that such 'really Christian' love is quite irrelevant to our life here on earth. Hostile commentators can only detect slavishness, and willingness to endorse evil, in such passivity. There have to be limits to self-abnegation: I cannot do what is asked of me if it goes against the command of God, and requires denial of God or injury to others. But how far may I co-operate when there is no immediate injury? Most Christians before Constantine maintained that they could not serve as soldiers, because they might have to kill someone, but that they should pay the taxes which maintained the armies and pray for the armies' success. Jesus's instruction, 'if someone tells you to go with him one mile, go with him two', in this familiar English version, disguises the Greek verb for commandeering transport (Matthew 5: 41). Did he mean that we should collaborate with an army of occupation, since its members are also children of God?

CIRCLES OF FRIENDSHIP

So some commentators think that there is a divinely-sanctioned form of 'friendship', which they like to call *agape*, and which amounts to total self-abnegation, and the denial of all ordinary forms of friendship. Sacrificial love does not discriminate between the merits of those it serves, nor think one consequence any better than another. Where it sees 'need' it acts, without concern for the future or for the disappointed expectations of those who cannot now be helped. On this account, any attempt to discriminate or to hold back amounts to egoism and a lack of faith. This is sometimes mistaken for universalism, but it is not the same ideal. The universalist's aim is to do as much good with one's time and energy as one possibly can, irrespective of personal love-liking, loyalty or shared ideals. Universalists are concerned with the good of all, and will prefer to act through large-scale and impersonal institutions. When they do acknowledge an obligation to help one particular person, it is because anyone ought to help that person, and ought to do so because helping her will serve the general good. The usual example given is the supposed duty to save a public benefactor rather than one's parent, child or spouse from a burning building – and the real duty, in any case, would be to promote fire safety regulations, not to spend energy on particular cases. An 'agapeistic' ethic has different implications.

> An ethic of undifferentiated love which allowed of no
> application to proximate relations could have little relevance
> for embodied human beings who can be in only one place at
> a time and must needs be closer to some people than others.
>
> (O'Donovan 1986: 240)

The sacrificial lover does not care what happens elsewhere, but only to do the task immediately assigned in the divine lottery. It remains possible, of course, that more immediately discernible friendships amount to just such divinely ordained duties – but if so, they are still to be fulfilled only out of faith in God, and not for the personal, shared satisfaction of the 'friends'.

> To join one's will to the will of God so that the human will
> consents to whatever the divine will prescribes, there being no
> other reason why it wants this or that, save that it knows God
> wants it; this is what it is to love God.
>
> (Aelred, *Mirror of Charity* 2: 18; Squire 1969: 37)

Other commentators, and probably the majority, prefer to see friendship, mediated through family ties and personal devotion, clans, clubs and colleges, as our best image of the 'lights lit at the festival of the peaceful Trinity' (Hopkins 1959: 197). It is not our business to abandon will and judgement in our friendly dealings. 'It is no excuse for sin, if you do it for a friend' (Squire 1969: 108). But neither is it righteous to disown one's friends on the plea that one thereby shows one's love of God: 'if you love not your brother whom you have seen, how can you love God whom you have not seen?' Jesus, after all, expressly denounced the Pharisaical judgement that one could dedicate something to God's service rather than use it to assist one's parents (Matthew 15: 3ff.). 'He that saith he is in the light, and hateth his brother, is in darkness even until now' (I John 2: 9).

Does it follow that one should prefer those immediate duties and attachments to more 'abstract' or 'distant' duties, such as those we owe to country or to humankind? 'Every real friendship is a sort of secession, even a rebellion' (Lewis 1963: 75). Christians before Constantine were accused of opting out, of living in little societies of friends, showing a praiseworthy concern for each other and for other cases of need, but forgetting that they also belonged to cities, an empire, the human race. Politicians nowadays quite often think that Christians should restrict their concerns like this, and not express inconvenient moral judgements on wider issues. But that restriction is another instance of being too much concerned with those who immediately 'belong', and forgetting that friendship extends to link individuals and groups into communities. *Pace* E. M. Forster (and Meilaender 1981: 81), Dante did not put Brutus and Cassius in the lowest circle of Hell because they had betrayed their personal friend rather than their country, but because they had betrayed their sworn duty to a divinely endorsed Emperor (as Dante believed), preferring the interests of their class to civil peace. Only when a country has ceased to be a community, linked by interconnected networks of friendship and by a shared vision of the good, do the smaller circles of friends become the true country. This is indeed to accept the ancient picture of civic friendship as the bond of peace: those theories of the state that see it merely as a device to enforce a truce between potentially warring strangers have already admitted that our primary loyalty is always to something smaller and more personal. To 'betray' that sort of state may be imprudent, but hardly treacherous.

Friendship, as a personal, civil and religious ideal, is a reminder that there is more to life than obedience to abstract law, or than a wish to 'do good' to all and sundry. True friendship, which is love purged of the wish to keep things for, and to, ourselves (see Burnaby 1967), comes in many forms, but all are united in the realization that if we would do good, we must do it in Blake's 'minute particulars':

> This is what the love of God consists in: the love of our neighbour. It is also written: 'this is my commandment that you love one another as I have loved you'. And how did the Lord love us? 'Greater love hath no man than this that he lay down his life for his friends.' And how will you lay down your life for me, if you will not lend me a needle and thread when I need it? How will you shed your blood for me, if you think it beneath you to give me a cup of cold water, if you cannot be bothered to take your hand out of your pocket for me? If you refuse to say a good word for me, when will you die for me? Let us, therefore, obey each other, love each other, for love is the fulfilling of the law.
>
> (Aelred: cited by Squire 1969: 59)

REFERENCES

Blake, W. (1966) *Complete Writings* (ed. G. Keynes), London: Oxford University Press.

Boswell, J. (1953) *Life of Johnson*, London: Oxford University Press.

Burnaby, J. (1967) 'Love' in J. Macquarrie (ed.) *A Dictionary of Christian Ethics*, London: SCM Press: pp. 197–200.

Clark, S. R. L. (1983) *The Nature of the Beast*, Oxford: Oxford University Press (1st ed. 1980).

——(1987) 'The city of the wise', *Apeiron* 20: 63–80.

Dwyer, J. (1987) *Virtuous Discourse*, Edinburgh: John Donald.

Edwards, J. (1969) *Charity and its Fruits*, (ed. T. Edwards), London: Banner of Truth Trust (1st ed. 1852).

Furnish, V. (1972) *The Love Command in the New Testament*, Nashville, Tennessee: Abingdon Press.

Hopkins, G. M. (1959) *Sermons and Devotional Writings* (ed. C. Devlin), London: Oxford University Press.

Lewis, C. S. (1957) *The Problem of Pain*, London: Fontana.

——(1963) *The Four Loves*, London: Fontana (1st ed. 1960).

McFague, S. (1987) *Models of God*, London: SCM Press.

Meilaender, G. (1981) *Friendship*, Notre Dame and London: University of Notre Dame Press.

Moffatt, J. (1929) *Love in the New Testament*, London: Hodder and Stoughton.

Mullett, M. E. (1988) 'Byzantium: a friendly society?' *Past and Present* 118: 3–24.

Nygren, A. (1932) *Agape and Eros* (tr. A. G. Herbert), London: SPCK.

O'Donovan, O. (1986) *Resurrection and Moral Order*, Leicester: Intervarsity Press.

Outka, G. (1972) *Agape: an Ethical Analysis*, New Haven and London: Yale University Press.

Peschke, C. H. (1978) *Christian Ethics*, Alcester and Dublin: C. Goodlife Neale.

Squire, A. (1969) *Aelred of Rievaulx*, London: SPCK.

Traherne, T. (1960) *Centuries*, Oxford: Clarendon Press.

Vaughan, J. (1983) *Sociality, Ethics and Social Change*, Lanham and London: University Press of America.

Chapter Three

FEMALE FRIENDSHIP

SUE LIMB

Female friendship seems to have reached a significant stage in its history. In 1987 Susie Orbach and Luise Eichenbaum published *Bittersweet: facing up to feelings of love, envy and competition in women's friendships.* After examining countless case histories of women born soon after the Second World War, they come to the conclusion that, in view of the social and cultural changes brought about in the past two decades, principally by the Women's Movement, women now have a chance to evolve their friendships beyond the stage of what they call 'merged attachment' – the kind of selfless caring and support which we shared, as infants, with our mothers. Now we can advance towards a model of friendship less glutinous, and more muscular. 'We have the opportunity to acknowledge our need for other women as well as our need for recognition and acceptance of our autonomous selves'(Orbach and Eichenbaum 1987: 174). I think I know what they mean.

I was born just after the Second World War, and I recognize in their analysis of women's friendship certain familiar syndromes. To explore these a little it might be useful to remember what it was like to grow up in the Fifties and Sixties, and to make friends from early childhood with others of the same sex. The dawning consciousness of our femaleness is also relevant here, since we are considering what makes female friendship distinct and unique. For me, the consciousness of my sex dawned like a day in dingy mid-December.

I was a girl. This was a disaster. My mother was a graduate, but that didn't alter her slave status in our household. None of her six brothers had attempted University education: they saw her as an aberration rather than a standard-bearer. A generation later, it was obvious to her daughter that boys and men were somehow innately more glamorous and important. Perhaps it was because of their adornment – secret, but none the less majestic for that. I prayed for a penis of my very own.

'Please, God,' I whispered, 'send me a boy's thingy. If you do, I promise I will be a good girl for ever and ever. Amen.'

The Almighty resisted this appeal, despite his taste for paradoxes. But I wasn't beaten yet. I would shrug off my destiny. I seized my shorts.

'Call me Norman,' I told my mother. 'I'm going to be a boy instead.' What exactly she did call me is not recorded. My dolls were all guys, too. Antony, Jeremy, Timothy, Christopher....it's a wonder they didn't found a fast-food empire in San Francisco. I climbed trees. I frowned. I rejected all the propaganda – the way we were all dressed in icing-sugar pink, adorned with confectioner's curls and bows and encouraged to be sweet and nice. I began to suspect that the highest goal a girl could aspire to was to become a kind of expensive cake. Our destiny was obviously to be devoured.

At Christmas, I played a shepherd boy in the school nativity play. My hair was cropped short, my shoulders were broad, my voice was deep.

'Christine Smith's mother said she thought you were really a boy,' reported my mother. I was dizzy with triumph. A boy! REALLY a boy! I'd never been nearer to realizing my fantasy. But one of my girl friends didn't think much of all this juvenile transvestism. She tried to coax me away from Marlon and towards Marlene.

'Look,' she pointed out instructively, 'at your Mother.'

At the time my mother was trotting daintily across the school yard (she was a teacher at my Primary School – another source of confusion). 'Look how she runs. She's really feminine. Why can't you be like that?'

By now I was nine, but still unconvinced about the desirability of the feminine. The crushing importance of the masculine principle in the culture was overwhelming. Who could possibly want to be a soft, spongy slave – or even a cake – when there was a chance of going POW ZAP TAKE THAT YOU BASTARD? I gazed at my mother's light, tripping figure in despair.

'The thing is, Christine,' I ventured, 'I wasn't really born a girl.'
'You what?!'
'Not many people know about this, but, well. . .I was born a boy.
And I had to have an operation.'

Christine grew wide-eyed. To this day I don't know if she
believed me. But I believed me. That was the important thing.

Apart from Christine's chastisements, I pursued my male
fantasy life unrebuked. It was a refuge from the daily scorn and
shame one was subjected to as a mere girl. You just couldn't escape
it: I was jeered at in the school yard ('Yeargh! Stupid GIRLS!'); at
home, where my big brother goaded me with my smallness and
femaleness until I lost my temper and smashed up his model
aeroplanes, whereat he lost his temper and drove a pencil quite
deep into my knee (I still have the scars); but above all, everywhere
one looked, in newspapers, books and magazines, on hoardings,
advertisements, at the cinema, the voice of the culture boomed
with all its mighty authority that the only thing for a girl to be was
pretty or good. Who would not rebel at such a milksop destiny?

The Famous Five, a children's book popular in this period,
includes a boy-girl character very similar to my youthful self. She
was known as George (short for Georgina) and she cut her hair
short and wore trousers and behaved like a boy in order to have
access to the exciting world of smugglers and spies whom the
Famous Five were forever tracking down. (In due course, I suspect,
they grew up and joined M.I.5.) This kind of transsexual aspiration
was the only way a girl could rebel against her sex, and was briefly
possible in those pre-puberty years before the body started its
treacherous capitulation to the other side.

There was one other refuge from tiresome femaleness, though
– a significant one. The moment I made my first real girl friend, I
stopped feeling the ache of alienation. Somehow, the company of
other little girls cancelled out the deprivations of femaleness.
There was solidarity in our friendship, and room to be active and
adventurous, to take initiatives and exercise aggression and
demonstrate high spirits. It was also, I discovered, quite soothing
to play quietly with dolls. I even developed a taste for those paper
mannequins whose wardrobes were constantly being changed by
means of paper tabs which folded over their shoulders. Yes, even
this most docile of female occupations began to exert a slight

fascination, as in the company of my girl friends I could for a moment suspend the struggle to deny my destiny and learn to take delight in clothes. I did not feel so horribly female with my girl friends. I just felt like a person. I could relax at last.

Girls' play traditionally explores fantasies about home, school, and hospitals, and often as we played and the boys roared past us on their bombing missions, or booted footballs mightily against the railings, I couldn't help feeling that their world was really very dull and brutal despite their having all the power and the glory. Bombs and balls! Yes, boys were very boring. With my girl friends I indulged all the impulses to be secret and clever. We wrote each other letters in code. We agonized over which school to send our dolls to. We slipped into a delicious variety of roles: *really strict* teachers, mysterious doctors and (in my case) masterful husbands. There was room, in our girls' universe, to be anything, to do anything, and to forget our Shirley Temple identity in the intoxication of action.

The hormones were stacked against us, though. Soon after I went to Secondary School the dreaded Menarche descended. Terrible word, isn't it? Sounds monstrous and totalitarian, somehow. And that's how it felt. More shame – bitter shame, and pain. My mother did not exactly welcome me into the sisterhood. 'Oh, No!' was her reaction. It seemed rather unfair to have a dirty little secret thrust upon you, with none of the naughty delight that should accompany it. That's being female for you. Shameful and besmirched without lifting a finger. Poor old Eve.

One day at school I had such terrible period pains that I had to grope my way along the walls to the school office, where I fainted on the floor. I was put to bed, my mother summoned, and the Headmistress herself came to sponge my fevered brow, without the source of these excruciating cramps ever being mentioned by any of the participants. It was a crazy world, growing up in the Fifties. It seems to me now a miracle that any of us are anything like sane.

And the disgustingness of periods drove me back desperately towards the male world I longed to enter. My girl friend of the time was another Christine, but a boy-girl like me with even gruffer manners. Hiding sanitary towels in our school bags was not our idea of fun. We wanted to be escaping from a prison camp, for goodness' sake. To distance ourselves from the whole thing, we turned it into a heroic British film of the post-war era. The period itself became the enemy, complete with code name, and all its tiresome paraphernalia were the ammunition – code-named too. I would flick a note across on to her desk in the middle of Biology. ZANZIBAR ON THE HORIZON, it would say. REQUEST TX 2s CAPTAIN BARBAROUS OVER. She was David Niven. I was Antony Quinn. We wouldn't give in without a struggle, dammit.

A girls' school is the perfect place for gender-bending. Here we could pretend that we weren't girls, because there were no tiresome males to measure ourselves against. Well, there was a Physics master or two, but they were awkward, bumbling creatures. Our school was a seraglio without a sultan: the Physics masters were its eunuchs. In this haven we could swim in unisex pleasure, enact unisex dramas and even indulge in unisex passion. Older girls, especially the tall, dark, handsome ones, became objects of obscure desire. One glimpse of the tennis captain, Lynne Wilson, and it was a hopeless case of Love Fifteen.

A flash of her dusky profile across a crowded quad, and my heart bounded in ecstasy. She noticed my prostration, and wrote me an encouraging letter (delivered to me – will I ever forget it? – in the balcony of the gymnasium). *You intrigue me and I like you*, she wrote, in strange loopy handwriting and rather curious turquoise ink. *Keep it up.* Keep it up? I ran out and bought some turquoise ink. I wrote loopy. I painted pictures of us playing tennis together. Boy, did I keep it up. But my fantasies were of a refined purity. I haven't the faintest idea, if I'd found myself suddenly alone in the changing-rooms with her, what I'd have wanted to do with her. Nothing, I think. Only gazing, as in John Donne's *The Extasie*: the poem in which Donne describes a mutual fascination so refined that all the lovers do is to lie side by side holding hands and gazing into each other's eyes:

> So to entergraft our hands, as yet
> Was all the meanes to make us one,
> And pictures in our eyes to get
> Was all our propagation.
> As 'twixt two equall Armies, Fate
> Suspends uncertain victorie,
> Our soules (which to advance their state,
> Were gone out,) hung 'twixt her, and mee.
>
> (Donne 1966: 75)

My soul was certainly gone out. And no subsequent adult passions ever matched these girlish crushes in intensity or purity.

My friend Christine shared in these devotions. Intimacy stoked up the secret fires. We kept a log of sightings. We copied details of dress and manners. I developed a Lynne Wilsonian drawl and amble. But at the same time, and without any sense of incongruity, we kindled at the sight upon our television screens, of various male matinée idols of the era. Christine was a sucker for the thin dark one in *Laramie*. Jess, I think his name was. I palpitated at the sight of Kookie in *77 Sunset Strip* – or was it Adam Faith? Both, probably. We were generous in our adoration, bestowing it impartially on man, woman, and, occasionally, tortoises. (Perhaps more research could be done on the importance of pets to the pubescent girl. Many gerbils and hamsters could testify to the intensity of maternal devotion lavished on them by their young owners.)

The fact was, no matter how perverse it all sounds, we had a great time. We were complete citizens of our universe, not mere girls. Safe in the sanctuary of our single-sex school, we did not have to endure the odium of comparisons with the unfair sex. Not surprisingly, one of my friends began to think with some longing of the nunnery, though once she got to University she thought the better of it and devoted herself instead to a devout promiscuity.

By now we were sour sixteen. Some minimal contact with the local boys' school was inevitable. In discussion groups we sat self-conscious, silenced by the glandular riot. I sweated right through my shirt and red blouse and blue blazer and ended up with red, white and blue armpits. It didn't help that our school uniform still confirmed our surrogate male status, with its collar and tie, v-neck jumper and dashing blazer. Underneath the male uniform, bizarrely enough, we all wore stockings and suspender belts. Later we were to realise that this was all very sexy. At the time it just seemed a fiendishly uncomfortable and absurd way to clothe your legs, ensuring that the tops of your thighs were forever encased in arctic frost. It was a torment reserved for women, of course. Men wore sensible trousers and shoes that actually kept the winter out.

Female friendship provided plenty of chances for revenge, though. The notes were still passed, only this time it was THAT ONE BY THE WINDOW LOOKS LIKE A DINOSAUR. . .SMELLS LIKE ONE, TOO. We may have been sweaty bondslaves, silenced by our lowly status, but by God we could be subversive. Men have always feared that women friends are laughing at them, from Aristophanes' *Lysistrata* (in which all the women of the town withhold their sexual favours from their husbands as a form of industrial action to protest against the wars) to Shakespeare's *The Merry Wives of Windsor*, in which jealous husbands and predatory philanderers are alike humiliated. Mirabel, the commanding man-about-town hero of Congreve's *The Way of the World*, will not embark upon marriage without setting out his terms: he hopes to forbid his fiancée the sardonic pleasures of female friendship: 'I covenant that your friendship be general; that you admit no sworn confidante, or intimate of your own sex; no she-friend to screen her affairs under your countenance, and tempt you to make trial of a mutual secrecy' (1974: 197).

This most useful function of female friendship – the alibi – was gradually revealed to us, except that it was parents we were gulling, not husbands. All the same, it was good practice. 'I was at Mary's,' many a slightly rumpled schoolgirl has reported, returning home late after an assignation in a dark corner of some seedy cafe. And of course, the sordid details of our trysts, and our swains, were faithfully reported to our bosom chums. For we inherited a splendid oral tradition that went back to the Wife of Bath: Chaucer's dazzling celebration of the much-married go-getter: a kind of medieval Zsa Zsa Gabor. She placed a high value on her female confidante, her 'gossip' as she called her:

> ...my gossib, dwelling in oure town,
> God hav hir soule! Hir name was Alisoune,
> She knewe myn herte and eek my privitee
> Bet than our parisshe-preest, so moot I thee!
> To hir biwreyed I my conseil al:
> For had myn housbonde pissed on a wal,
> Or doon a thing that sholde had coste his lyf
> To hir, and to another worthy wyf
> And to my nece, which that I loved weel,
> I wolde had tolde his conseil every-deel.

(My confidante, Alison, God Bless her! – she lived nearby, and she knew my most intimate thoughts, much better than our parish priest. I poured out my heart to her, and to another of our neighbours, and also to my favourite niece: they knew every little secret about my

husband. Whether he'd committed some capital crime, or just pissed against a wall, they were always the first to know.)

(Chaucer 1962: 572)

The curious thing about female friendship as we experienced it in our teenage years, in the early Sixties, was its spaciousness. There was room in it to be subversive and satirical towards males. But if we wanted to suspend the sex-war for a moment and dip a toe in dalliance, then we could relish the details afterwards in feverish *reportage* with our girl friends (and this de-briefing afterwards was often more delicious than the peccadillo itself). Moreover, there was still plenty of room for shared fantasy.

Whatever credulous males may think, the fantasies of schoolgirls do not revolve exclusively around mere marriage and babies. I suppose I must have turned over the odd routine daydream about marrying one or other of my matinée idols (though none of the local schoolboys, thank you very much) but at sixteen the fictions I spun with my new best friend Mary, and which we explored in a jointly-written epic hundreds of pages long, scorned such lowly scenarios as love and marriage. We had discovered idealism.

Mary was of a religious cast of mind, and figured in this narrative as a trouble-shooting nun, bringing food and spiritual enlightenment to the Third World under the UN flag. And me? I was the UN Secretary-General herself, of course, and much too busy for any hanky-panky (although a gangling Norwegian Aide called Olaf did hang adoringly around my helicopter and supervised my briefs). Between us, we did a hell of a lot of good work out there in the Third World, though I say so myself.

Whether male friendship in the teenage years offers such an infinite variety of experience, I cannot conjecture. But the male codes of behaviour in those days were pretty relentless, and I can't imagine the boys having quite such a good time as we did, even though, paradoxically, they were in the driving seat when it came to almost anything to do with the outside world, including driving. I imagine that for a lot of boys who were our contemporaries, suffering in silence filled most of their time. There were so very few feelings they could admit to, and to whom could they admit them, in any case? The very sound of *shared intimacies* resonates with indecency. Indeed, intimacy, the state of being heart-to-heart in which we girls rejoiced, meant also sexual congress in the gutter newspapers of the day, and probably in the consciousness of most boys.

Their horror of being thought homosexual was overwhelming. Whereas we girls all knew we were, or at least had been recently, as bent as hairpins. I don't think I've got Lynne Wilson entirely out of my system to this day – a suspicion reinforced recently when I read, not without an answering tremor, a noble poem by Clive James entitled *Bring Me the Sweat of Gabriela Sabatini* (James 1987) – a celebration of the erotic power of the tawny tennis captain.

Still, all the vicarious variety of this tropical teenage existence had to come to an end. I went to University. Here I made new girl friends, but somehow the fantasy element dropped away. You didn't need fantasy in Cambridge: it was quite weird enough as it was. I was no longer Antony Quinn or the UN Secretary-General. I was a woman – well, by my standards, anyway. And that in itself was strange enough to be going on with.

Trying to make sense of literature was my nominal occupation, but any fool could see that falling in love was the serious business of the day. This was before the first inklings of feminism, I might add, but it was fairly inevitable, I think, that we should dedicate much of our time to Eros. For the first time we were free, surrounded by large numbers of the opposite sex, and we had burst like butterflies from the dark sexless carapaces of our blazers. We buzzed in the sunshine and fed deep upon the nectar.

These were the Romantic years. Courtship needs its confidantes, as many a dramatist and novelist has discovered, and now like the best friends Rosalind and Celia, exiled in the forest in Shakespeare's *As You like It*, we talked one another through endless fallings-in-love and out again at the other side. Nor was this the soggy, uncritically supportive 'merged attachment' outlined in *Bittersweet*. We could be as sharp and sceptical as Celia reacting to Rosalind's rhapsodies about her dashing sweetheart Orlando:

'But have I not cause to weep?' [enquires Rosalind, when Orlando is late for a date].
'As good a cause as one would desire; therefore weep,' [answers Celia]. . . .
'But why did he swear he would come this morning, and comes not?'

'Nay, certainly, there is no truth in him'. . . .
'Not true in love?'
'Yes, when he is in, but I think he is not in.'
(Shakespeare 1975: 85)

And so on. This crisp and critical reaction to Rosalind's state is part teasing, and does not mean that Celia is not being, in the sacred jargon of our time, *caring* and *supportive*. She is simply being caring and supportive and intelligently playful. I experienced much the same teasing attention from my female friends. For example, I distinctly recall breaking the news to a girl friend that I was about to announce my engagement to a man whose towering intelligence was somewhat marred, in her view, by his toadlike appearance and proletarian croak.

'Oh, no!' she screamed. 'Not him!'

I couldn't agree: being enchanted, I saw the prince beneath the warts. The conflict between female friend and male partner had set in.

It is a continuing story, and there are many day-to-day conflicts of loyalty to resolve, for most women: between the demands of husbands and children and the need for female company. *Bittersweet* chronicles the difficulty even the most emancipated women have in juggling their domestic obligations to make room for time with female friends. But no woman of sense gives up her independent friendships with other women. They can be her greatest help and support.

What exactly is the nature of this supportiveness? I think it varies, in Britain, according to class. Working-class women have traditionally relied on friends and neighbours to share the domestic burdens: taking turns to care for children, invalids and old people, attending confinements and assuaging griefs. For women on the treadmill of domestic labour, the wifely conviviality of the back-to-back rows of houses in industrial towns must have provided a lifeline: a sense of solidarity as well as simple practical help. One gets a glimpse of this world in novels from Mrs Gaskell to D. H. Lawrence.

A price had to be paid for membership of this club, however. Any woman who aspired to education as a means of escape was likely to arouse suspicion and hostility. Though they could be subversive and jocular in their private attitudes to men, most working women supported the patriarchal status quo, either from religious conviction or with a certain jaundiced fatalism. They might want a better destiny than the coal-mine for their sons, but for their daughters anything other than marriage would be unthinkable. Theirs was the solidarity of slaves.

It was at least solidarity, though. And it offered a lifeline which has snapped, now young wives find themselves isolated on suburban housing estates, out of touch perhaps with their home town and childhood friends. In the Migraine Trust's newsletter I often see heart-rending advertisements from young mothers with two or more small children asking for help when migraine strikes. As our society has become more mobile, and we are segregated from our old folk and our handicapped and even from our neighbours by higher and higher hedges of *Cupressus Leylandii*, the tradition of caring for one's female friends has dwindled. More often than not, they live hundreds of miles away. I live in Gloucestershire, now; my best friends live in Cambridge, London and Yorkshire.

This geographical dislocation merely reinforces the change in the function of female friendship among the middle classes. Supportiveness is not, now, so much a matter of sharing domestic duties, as of discussing experience and sustaining one another in the minefield of decisions that are the privilege of the educated middle-class woman. To marry or not? To have a child or not, and if so, when? To change one's job? To change one's political loyalties or religious beliefs?

At the moment, for example I feel I am deep in several continuing conversations, conducted by letter and phone and at occasional meetings. For example, I try to encourage one friend to recover from a failed marriage and from the shattering cruelties she has suffered. When at last she falls in love again, I rejoice, I meet him, I tell her he is indeed splendid, and will still be splendid to the dispassionate observer long after Eros's sleepless fevers have given way to dozy domesticity. At the same time I warn her not to give up her work or friends or home altogether on the tide of this first fine careless rapture.

In the past she helped me through similar experiences: mourned with me the end of a relationship, though carefully reminding me that there were good reasons why it had to end, and so on. The peculiar nature of female friendship, for me, is this mixture of sympathy and instruction: of a loving heart and a shrewd eye. And above all it offers an endless patience and curiosity, so that feelings that may be buried and yet irritating can be brought to light, explored, and, one hopes, dispersed. Some men may enjoy this kind of laundering of the soul with their close friends, but I suspect it is as rare in the male world as it is commonplace in the female.

Our friends see us at our most vulnerable, know us intimately over the years, and best understand whether what we are currently saying or doing is making sense. In other words, I think female friends help us to cultivate our integrity and guard against losing our way. This is, of course, most likely to happen under the influence of Eros.

One of the useful enigmas of falling in love is that one's female friends remain undeluded. They provide footholds of sound sense to help one away from disaster. They patiently endure all the significant details of the affair, providing encouragement, solace and congratulation where needed. And as the authors of *Bittersweet* point out, they must accept that their newly-enamoured friend will perforce spend less time with them. I think most of us understand this mechanism, though it is hard when one woman gets married leaving her girl friend still single and feeling bereft and neglected. But as we get older, a new truth breaks in upon us – that after all, female friendship and love between man and woman are very different things, and that whilst any number of Eros's arrows fall away into the dust, their darts spent, and their feathers frazzled, female friendship endures.

Eros makes the heart bound: we rush to our mirrors and see a special face there: captivated, captivating. We open ourselves with careful artifice, aching to be more fascinating than we are, and inspired by adrenalin, achieving it. Friendship, in contrast, cares not if we have combed our hair, or if we feel dull and uninspired. In friendship we open ourselves with careless honesty. If our lover's laugh is irritating, it is a moment of intense, though infinitesimal damage. Our friend's laugh is welcome whatever its sound. Friendship escapes the desperate distorting appetites of Eros, and survives.

For this reason I cannot venture into lesbian love, as so many feminists have done, or see it as a logical extension of female friendship. 'For many women,' write Orbach and Eichenbaum, 'closeness with a woman and the intimacy she finds in her friendship is deeply sustaining' (Orbach and Eichenbaum 1987: 9). Many women, they say, now allow the erotic side of their feelings for other women to emerge. But I have always felt uneasy when such feelings surface in my friendships with women. I have an instinct to preserve my female friendships intact and protect them from the aches and trickeries of Eros.

A very dear friend of mine occasionally reminds me that she is in love with me, and always I am reduced to a speechless, queasy sense that that way madness lies – that everything that I value about her company, and love about her as a human being, would be threatened if we were to slide on to that slippery slope where longing can so quickly turn to loathing. After such affairs, with the inevitable feeling of *omnia tristia*, how could we recapture the unspoilable ordinariness of our original interest in each other – which, if left unmolested, will surely sustain us to the grave.

Female friendships are lifelong. Another woman friend, for example, I have known for thirty-three of my forty-one years – since the days when I played the Shepherd Boy in the Nativity play (she played the angel). Though most of us have grown out of any notions of Mr Right, once a man has been tarnished with a certain amount of wrong, he has to go to make way for another, probably worse, candidate. The mating game is, in our society at least, still inexorably consecutive; whereas friendships are plural and elastic. Nobody expects her female friend to fulfil all her important physical, emotional and intellectual needs. With one's girl friends, the pressure's off. So the marriages explode like fireworks: whilst friendships glow fitfully, like banked-up bonfires, on and on into the night.

Goldsmith understood this, observing that friendship was a disinterested commerce between equals whereas love was an abject intercourse between tyrants and slaves. The element of equality in female friendship is an important one, indeed, though feelings of envy and competition inevitably emerge. I envy one friend her youthful looks; another, her freedom from the need to work; another, her single footloose status and the travels she enjoys. But I assume that they in turn probably envy me what good fortune has brought me. I too have blessings to count.

We are all of us, it seems to me, visited by Dame Fortune. She spins her wheel: it is your turn to grieve: later it will be mine. We take it in turns to support and care for our female friends. As we reach middle age, some of us have to reconcile ourselves to a future without children, despite having wanted them. Many of my friends are facing this dilemma now: I only missed it myself by a whisker. Conquering feelings of envy and accepting the nature of our own lot can be hard, but time helps, and so does acknowledging one's difficulties, as Orbach and Eichenbaum point out.

Their Women's Therapy Centres in London and New York have helped many women to come to grips with the negative feelings that can well up within friendship. Women are used to tensions and disappointments in love, but less so in friendship, and Orbach and Eichenbaum are surely right to encourage us to speak out to purge bad feeling. I'm not as convinced as they are, however, that women ever entirely abandoned this healthy candour. There are times when we do not need to be supported, but plunged back down to reality with a healthy bump.

One of the useful achievements of the Women's Movement, though, has been to legitimize what we have always known in our hearts: that female friendships are the most vital of life-support systems. Shakespeare certainly understood this and played with the idea in *The Merry Wives of Windsor*:

> *Mrs Ford*: Mistress Page! Trust me, I was going to your house.
> *Mrs Page*: And trust me, I was coming to you.
>
> (Shakespeare 1942: 57)

'I think,' comments Ford sourly to Mrs Page, 'if your husbands were dead, you two would marry' (1942:65). It is typical of a man to see women's friendship as aspiring to the condition of marriage. In fact, most marriages would benefit enormously from learning to cultivate the traditional strengths of friendship. In these days of brief marriage, friendship is more than ever becoming recognized as the bedrock of society.

The delight, repose and stimulus which we first gained from each other's company as small girls, continues over the decades and springs afresh with every new friendship formed. I do not wish to suggest that women are never maddened or betrayed by their female friends: they are, but such experiences are rare, and my own history of female friendship has been perhaps my most reliable source of pleasure. Certainly it provides me with the best sense I have of who I am – and my most likable sense of myself.

Every woman worth knowing makes this valuable discovery, and the best of men understand it and envy us for it. Dr Johnson yearned for 'the endearing elegance of female friendship': Shakespeare celebrated it in his comedies, and in his darker moments showed, in Charmian and Iras, Paulina and Emilia, how female loyalty could inspire tremendous bravery, even to the dagger's point.

It is a mistake to think that female friendship has not been valued and recognized in past times: Janet Todd's *Women's Friendship in Literature* explores the enormous range of material in the eighteenth century alone. Twentieth century women may detect a familiar feeling in Mme de Stael's letters to Mme Recamier: 'You have made me know all that is really sweet about love for a woman – it is the alliance of two weak creatures who face their oppressors together' (Todd 1980: 393). *La lutte continue . . .* but the female protagonists nowadays are armed by feminism. We are stronger as individuals, less dependent on men for our sense of ourselves, and emancipated from and hostile to many brutal and competitive values which have deformed male-dominated society. Our friendships are bound to gain in strength and become a positive force for grass-roots change, which as every gardener knows, is a most tenacious form of growth.

It is with the words of a wise gardening woman that I wish to end: a passage from *The Enchanted April* by Elizabeth von Arnim. It is a book which above all celebrates female friendship – the joy it brings, and its power to civilize and attune, in an almost Shakespearean way, spirits made ragged by disappointment and loneliness. Mrs Lotty Wilkins and Mrs Rose Arbuthnot discover a delightful rapport with each other, and despite husbandly disapproval, hire an Italian castle on the coast to share for the month of April.

Financial need forces them to advertise for two other ladies to join them, and the strangers seem at first disconsolate and disagreeable. One is a sulky young woman, sick of the beauty with which she is burdened. The other is an old woman, Mrs Fisher, who takes refuge in sour superiority to hide her vulnerability. Soon the young woman melts and smiles and is drawn into friendship, but old Mrs Fisher is a harder nut to crack.

Lotty Wilkins is equal to the challenge, however. A mad, impetuous creature, overflowing with infectious life-energy, she first inspires in Mrs Fisher nothing more than distaste and suspicion. But Lotty Wilkins, with a woman's intuition, understands what the old woman needs, and storms her barricades like the most dashing hero of Romantic Fiction:

> The look on her face gave Mrs Wilkins's heart a little twist when she saw it. 'Poor old dear,' she thought, all the loneliness of age flashing upon her, the loneliness of having outstayed one's welcome in the world. . .the complete loneliness of the old childless woman who has failed to make friends. It did seem that people could only be really happy in pairs – any sorts of pairs, not in the least necessarily lovers, but pairs of friends, pairs of mothers and children, and brothers and sisters – and where was the other half of Mrs Fisher's pair going to be found?
>
> Mrs Wilkins thought she had perhaps better kiss her again. The kissing in the afternoon had been a great success: she knew it, she had instantly felt Mrs Fisher's reaction to it. So she crossed over and bent down and kissed her and said cheerfully, 'We've come in –' which indeed was evident. This time Mrs Fisher actually put up her hand and held Mrs Wilkins's cheek against her own – this living thing, full of affection, of warm, racing blood; and as she did this she felt safe with this strange creature. . . .
>
> Mrs Wilkins was. . .delighted. 'I believe I'm the other half of her pair,' flashed into her mind. 'I believe it's me, positively me, going to be fast friends with Mrs Fisher!'
>
> . . .'Where are the others?' asked Mrs Fisher. 'Thank you – dear,' she added, as Mrs Wilkins put a footstool under her feet, a footstool obviously needed, Mrs Fisher's legs being short.
>
> 'I see myself throughout the years,' thought Mrs Wilkins, her eyes dancing, 'bringing footstools to Mrs Fisher. . .'
>
> (Arnim 1987: 358–9)

That's what female friendship offers: the pot of gold at the end of the rainbow, without the shadow of a shadow of a doubt. The real thing. The happy ending.

REFERENCES

Arnim, E. von (1986) *The Enchanted April*, London: Virago.

Chaucer, G. (1962) 'The Wyf of Bath's Prologue', in *The Complete Works*, edited by W. W. Skeat, London: Oxford University Press.

Congreve, W. (1974) *The Way of the World*, in *Four English Comedies*, Harmondsworth: Penguin.

Donne, J. (1966) 'The Extasie', in *The Metaphysical Poets*, edited by H. Gardner, Harmondsworth: Penguin.

Goldsmith, O. (1768) *The Good Natured Man.*

James, C. (1987) 'Bring me the sweat of Gabriela Sabatini', in *The London Review of Books* vol. 9, no. 16.

Johnson, S. (1759) *Rasselas.*

Orbach, S. and Eichenbaum, L. (1987) *Bittersweet: Facing up to Feelings of Love, Envy and Competition in Women's Friendships*, London: Century.

Shakespeare, W. (1975) *As You Like It*, in *The Arden Shakespeare*, edited by A. Lathaun, London: Methuen.

——(1942) *The Merry Wives of Windsor*, in *The Complete Works*, edited by J. Craig, London: Oxford University Press.

Todd, J. (1980) *Women's Friendship in Literature*, New York: Columbia University Press.

Chapter Four

MALE FRIENDS

MICHAEL NEVE

The *dialectics* of friendship. The title of this collection gives us aid, in thinking about male friendship, and helps emphasize that friendship between men is both changeable (friends will arrive, friends will disappear) and also a form of work. This working side of the dialectics of friendship promises a way out of the static idea of friendship as either a kind of social work, or a form of exhausted romanticism, with the libidinal undercurrent gone dead. The social work aspect (now made prominent by AIDS and the need for friendly assistance) is on display in Stuart Miller's *Men and Friendship*, a sweet-natured attempt to explore friendship and rivalries between men, that doesn't state a principle, and as a result makes its author into a kind of visitor, the friend who 'calls' on others to see how they are doing (Miller 1983). Miller doesn't make his investigation part of his dialectic, as it were, and the book leaves no trace of what the grounds for friendship might be. Likewise, the writer Michael Ignatieff, reviewing books on love for *The Times Literary Supplement*, sees friendship as important, but as a kind of diminuendo (Ignatieff 1988). We have friends, he says, some old, some new. But, because the most trusted are our old friends, there isn't much left to say: we exercise a sad wisdom in engaging with them, enjoying (just about) an unillusioned, familiar story-telling. Not much of a dialectic there.

But male friendship must partake of the rhythms, the exits and entrances, the highs and lows, of life itself. As Sue Limb suggests in the previous chapter, women help each other survive men, not just once, but as a form of vigilant work that runs through a life. Men do the same (within 'heterosexual' life) and the dialectics of friendship are partly based on the idea of a permanent life of

62

engagement (between the sexes in this example), most of which will bring change and difficulty, visibility and invisibility. One proposition that this short essay will set down is this: the man who sees himself as free of interpretative needs, supplied by others, has no friends.

Friendship, male friendship, cannot be so weak as to be unable to admit to weakness. It must be based on an 'adult' admission that the world is various and strange, and that fantasies of omnipotence, so strong for children, make friendship an impossibility. And it's not just an idea about not needing friends, but of not having any. They can't be had, because the omnipotent ideal has not yet allowed the child to become father to the man. Most male imbecility, and a peculiar form of male loneliness, comes from the idea that not to claim self-sufficiency as real is weak, or 'womanly'. As the child psychoanalyst Adam Phillips has suggested, men sometimes find other men the only acceptable form of women, and the relationship between men – its friendliness – helps make safe heterosexual anxieties. The quality of male friendship reveals the imagined deficiency in a displaced form. Shakespeare, that mysterious pimp, dwelling between the sexes, sees this, in the *Sonnets*, and in *Antony and Cleopatra* and *Hamlet*. Antony has no friends, not even Cleopatra, because of the massive demands on the idea of self-sufficiency that, as a soldier, he has to acknowledge. Hamlet, on the other hand, seen as weak or vacillating, has a different kind of loneliness. He is lonely in the presence of one of the truest friends in literature, Horatio. Without Horatio, there would be no play, no sense of Hamlet, whereas the generous but friendless Antony ends up puzzled and lost, calling all sorts of people he's never met properly 'friend'. And it's striking how Horatio never changes his feelings towards Hamlet (which allows him to listen to every word of his friend, without boredom or intrusion) when Hamlet travels far into a world of sexual confusion and political darkness. Hamlet never achieves royalty, it is true, and in that sense does not have to throw over his Falstaff, as does Prince Hal, in *Henry IV Part II* and *Henry V*. But part of the quality of Horatio's devotion to Hamlet is its lack of competitive exchange through the language of omnipotence. Unlike many commentators on *Hamlet* the play, Horatio sees that interior of Hamlet's wherein lies a heroic, terrible strength, of which Denmark is unworthy.

One sophisticated riposte at this point might be to take up (partly from Claude Lévi-Strauss) the idea that all these boys and men can get along with their heroics, and their friendships, because women (and girls) are simply ways in which men speak to each other. Thus, there might be something pernicious and harmful in the 'man who can admit to weakness', and thereby has male friends who help him along, because women pay the price for this admission by becoming signs flashed from man to man, signs that get used and then discarded. I take it that a great deal of one's doubts about Shelley turn on precisely this question. He has the friendship of Byron, but what about the treatment of Claire Clairmont? This idea, of a fundamental 'homosocial desire' that makes women part of the communicative domination being exercised by men who are in fact attracted to each other, has been explored by Eve Kosofsky Sedgwick in *Between Men: English Literature and Male Homosocial Desire* (Sedgwick 1985). Sedgwick's is a convoluted account but she can make one wonder about the homosocial, not the homosexual, in such texts as Laurence Sterne's *A Sentimental Journey*. In that book especially, servant girls are simply agents of sexual anecdote, even numerology, which men list for each other, a process that culminates in works outside Sedgwick's discussion, most famously Mozart's opera *Don Giovanni* and the exchange between the Don and Leporello: '*mille e tre*'.

Here, then, the man who one might admire most comes to a decision about male friendship that at first sight seems rather harsh: that it might itself be a kind of trap, since much of the language of such male friendship will be derogatory banter, and exchange, about used women. Here, the good man decides to have no friends, shunning the 'troops of friends' of the honest man who admits to weakness, but who then abuses women, and talks about it.

Before proceeding further, something must be said about male homosexuality, in that I am proposing that male friendship is at least in part a negotiation of the more general negotiations to do with women. My own view is that male homosexual friendship might as easily sustain itself in the facing of the experience of male homosexual lust (or love) as anything similar in the heterosexual world. Indeed the exhausted tone of those sexually-based distinctions can be exemplified by pointing out that male homosexual politics, in the 1890s and thereafter, took friendship to be cordial and sustaining without any need to embarrass itself with the distinctions founded on sexually reticent, perhaps hostile, heterosexual men. The world of Edward Carpenter, the world of Walt Whitman or J. A. Symonds, is a world of male friendship that does not present itself as the conundrum that it can be for heterosexual men. But it was also a world of intense hostilities and disagreements. The foundations for long friendship between homosexual men might – indeed must – be based on the same abnegation of the fantasy of self-sufficiency, and the same discovery of a weakness that is not exploitative, as any other kind of friendship. Indeed, my own experience is that homosexual men have heterosexual men friends, who help them, without any impingement or alteration in sexual orientation, and without understating the distinct world of homosexual experience. Whatever else homosexuals may be, they are no nicer than anyone else, and no less in need of the alternative conversation, the conversation that can only be had with someone who can explain the missing conversation with the loved one.

But this is prolix, and it is time to look at a body of work that takes a much harder look at friendship and, in both male and female voices, won't be bullied into thinking of it as easy or out of thinking of it as false. First, in a mild but determined essay, the Romantic writer Charles Lamb makes the point that one may actually have friends and not want to see them. His short piece entitled 'Many Friends' of 1825 (Lamb 1985: 254–6) makes friends into interruptions. They come, at the end of the day, in the middle of the meal, and pretend that there are things to say. Lamb longs for solitude, 'a Lodge in some vast Wilderness'. Lamb contrasts interestingly with Thomas de Quincey, who made himself desperate in trying to become Wordsworth's friend. And Lamb also leads into a great body of literature – Victorian poetry – that looks at friendship and its supposed virtues with an even more doubting gaze.

Secondly, in the disturbing and thematically courageous *New Oxford Book of Victorian Verse*, the editor, Christopher Ricks, realizes the poetry of the Victorian age in new and impressive directions (Ricks 1987). It may be reductionist to pick out central themes in this collection, but the reader cannot fail to be reawakened to the Victorian poetic idea that if God is dead, if Christ is not risen, and if love is lost, then friendship is likewise a stranger to a now ghostly (and ghastly) world. These voices, of dead poets, keep alive by speaking of the truths of death: the death of love, the death of friendship. Alfred Tennyson is great in all this, but this fine poem of friendship, male friendship, makes its discoveries where they are to be made, among the dead; Tennyson's friend Edward FitzGerald's translation of the 'Quatrains' of Omar Khayyam were much praised, and Tennyson writes to FitzGerald in the year that was to be FitzGerald's last (1883):

> A planet equal to the sun
> which cast it, that large infidel
> Your Omar; and your Omar drew
> Full-handed plaudits from our best
> In modern letters, and from two,
> Old friends outvaluing all the rest,
> Two voices heard on earth no more;
> But we old friends are still alive,
> And I am nearing seventy-four,
> While you have touch'd at seventy-five,
> And so I send a birthday line
> Of greeting.

FitzGerald (who liked to call his friends 'Boys') is praised by friends from beyond the grave. And elsewhere, Victorian poets strike a powerful note of disbelief – disbelief in the claims of love and friendship – particularly, and strikingly, Christina Rossetti. The astonishing innovations in Victorian verse – the dramatic monologue, and nonsense-verse – must come from some sense of the deadness of easy claims about love and friendship (Haughton 1988). Childe Roland comes to the Dark Tower; the Baker vanishes in *The Hunting of the Snark*; and the Dorset poet William Barnes can even make light of these dark things:

> 'False Friends-Like'
> When I wer still a bwoy, an' mother's pride,
> A bigger bwoy spoke up to me so kind-like,
> 'If you do like, I'll treat ye wi' a ride
> In thease wheel-barrow here.' Zoo I wer blind-like
> To what he had a-worken in his mind-like,
> An' mounted vor a passenger inside;
> An' comen to a puddle, perty wide,
> He tipp'd me in, a-grinnen back behind-like.

Zoo when a man do come to me so thick-like,
An' sheäke my hand, where woonce he pass'd me by,
An' tell me he would do me this or that,
I can't help thinken o' the big bwoy's trick-like.
An' then, vor all I can but wag my hat
An' thank en, I do veel a little shy.

Ricks's selection makes an old idea of Victorian male friendship
(that it could only be retrospective, because of repressions and
longings for death) seem tired and wrong. By choosing poems that
make more of death and its truths, the editor shows the Victorian
poets to be sceptical and unillusioned, but also terrifically alive to
the possibilities that, for example, love is real. But if it is not real,
then these poets do not wish for excuses. Male friendship, in this
anthology, keeps a religious consciousness – that one's male
friends may be like (and of course unlike) Christ – while not
forgetting that the death of such friends is the last place for
sentimentalism. Indeed the 'obsession with death' increasingly
appears, for the great Victorians, to be a poetical contribution –
the voice of the dead – towards a possible future state.

The Victorian poets, many of them, had the courage to be
without friends, and to see the friendless state as the true condition
of the world without God. Late Victorians – above all A. E.
Housman – can be thought of as writing almost permanently about
male friendship (and sexual struggle) but all Housman's male
friends are dead, or dying (but at least his 'lads' are sometimes
friends, sometimes soldiers who have died). For Housman, the
attractions of friendship, male friendship, were less powerful than
the pain that would come from friendship's failure. The hellish
stoicism of Housman contradicts even the doubts of Tennyson: for
Housman, poetic energy was entirely given up to the detailed
experience of it being better never to have loved, and lost, than
never to have loved at all. The death of friends, the death of
friendship, means something, for these writers: something
irreplaceable has died, or failed, and the dialectics of friendship
are dead too. Man, the 'unhappy tourist', to use an expression
made of the poet A. H. Clough, becomes also a stranger to his own
life, with a determined refusal to allow liberal optimism a chance
to pretend that it can all come back, in a recovery of social feeling
that replicates the past. The brave thought looks elsewhere, as in
section L of *In Memoriam*, 'Be near me when my light is low':

Be near me when my light is low,
When the blood creeps, and the nerves prick
And tingle; and the heart is sick,
And all the wheels of Being slow.

Be near me when the sensuous frame
Is rack'd with pangs that conquer trust;
And Time, a maniac scattering dust,
And Life, a Fury slinging flame.

Be near me when my faith is dry,
And men the flies of latter spring,
That lay their eggs, and sting and sing
And weave their petty cells and die.

Be near me when I fade away,
To point the term of human strife,
And on the low dark verge of life
The twilight of eternal day.

I said at the beginning that the man who sees himself as free of interpretative needs, who believes in his self-sufficiency at all points (psychological, and not just practical) has no friends. The Victorian poets doubt the trustworthiness of other voices and opinions and, in a Godless world, accept the death of friendship. They thus provide a model for the friendless life as the true life, the life that doesn't pretend that things haven't died. But the dialects and dialectics of friendship may have life in them yet, and male friendship may have other foundations. What might these be?

Aristotle, in his *Ethics*, and Cicero in his *De Amicitia*, set out the famous case that the basis for male friendship is a non-sexual relationship, based on equality (especially of rank), with mutual regard for simplicity of heart, good manners, and conversation. Cicero firmly believed that 'true friendship can only be found among the virtuous' and must be based on complete frankness (Cicero 1909: 170–215). Cicero's highly influential views were kept alive in the Middle Ages, and went on being recovered and found valuable in the age of Edward Gibbon. Manly love, male friendship, remains apart from fleshly love through to Montaigne

('Truly the name of brother is a beautiful name'), to Shelley, even to the nineteenth-century, privately homosexual writers, such as J. A. Symonds. And, in the nineteenth-century public school, the addition of physicality (via games) in fact becomes a form of male *adolescent* friendship: indeed, one might think of the adolescent as the youth who has nothing but male friends, having not yet undergone the strangeness of heterosexual experience and the recovery of male friendship within the negotiated world of women and adulthood. These worlds of permanent friendship and extravagant manifestation are distant from the reticent friendships of adulthood: in the eighteenth century, Johnson making his possible friendship for Boswell believable by never discussing it; or, from twentieth-century literature, Sherlock Holmes and Doctor Watson sharing one or two moments of unsought intimacy. As Jeffrey Richards and Owen Dudley Edwards have splendidly brought out, the cocaine-fuelled, remote asexuality of Holmes breaks down in *The Three Garridebs*, a story of 1925 (Richards 1987: 110). Killer Evans shoots Watson, who then experiences the epiphany within their many years of male friendship:

> My friend's wiry arms were around me and he was leading me
> to a chair. 'You're not hurt, Watson? For God's sake, say that
> you are not hurt!' It was worth a wound – it was worth many
> wounds – to know the depth of loyalty and love which lay
> behind that cold mask. The clear, hard eyes were dimmed for
> a moment and the firm lips were shaking. For the one and
> only time I caught a glimpse of a great heart as well as a great
> brain. All my years of humble but single-minded service
> culminated in that moment of revelation.
> 'It's nothing, Holmes. It's a mere scratch.'

These reticences and these small revelations, which are unostentatious, not easily brought into any sexual reading, and which feel true, are no doubt the heart of male friendship. The mutual feelings last over time, are free of the extravagance that can always come to seem empty, and they contain a sense of empathy between male friends, a sense of ordinary trust, that cannot but reveal itself at moments of danger or death.

The difficulty of thinking of friendship between men as

empathetic is that empathy may involve too much projection, too much unexamined projection which can seem like empathy. Empathy, no doubt an admirable thing, might have too many hidden wishes, some of them not quite what they might be, to be the source of true friendship. (One thinks of the nineteenth-century critic Sainte-Beuve, who 'empathized' with his friend Charles Baudelaire, but, partly *because* Baudelaire was his friend, thought his poems and essays to be inferior.) And one of the difficulties with taking empathy to be a source of friendship is that it continues the tradition of thinking of friendship between men as asexual, the opposite of the carnal, the Ciceronian alternative to the sexual connection. Instead, it might be worth asking whether the dialectics of male friendship aren't firmly rooted in an idea of the sexual characteristics of one's male friends, characteristics which, in acknowledging, even admiring, don't require a buried homosexual foundation to be real or authentic. Isn't the picturing of a male friend's sexual beauty part of the negotiation of the world (and of women) that the Ciceronian model doesn't quite deal with?

Trying to put this case together isn't easy, but valuable assistance can be gained from an unlikely quarter: aesthetic theory, theories about painting and its power, not least those expounded by Richard Wollheim in his mandarin but sensually charged book, *Painting as an Art* (Wollheim 1987). This book has many theses, some of them informed by psychoanalytic theory, and it takes great care to think about the media of art – oil paint, canvases – such that invoking it to ponder male friendship may seem perverse. But one of its proposals may help in thinking how we picture our friends aesthetically and sexually, and how this picturing helps form our friendship.

Especially in his discussion of single-figure paintings by Manet, and by Ingres, Wollheim suggests that one way of understanding the force, the art, of these works is that there is no singular relationship in them between the picture itself and the viewer of it as he or she walks around the gallery. Wollheim proposes that the expressive content in these pictures is there because as it were inside the picture, between the art-work and the gallery visitor, is an unseen viewer. The figures in the painting are being seen, or interrupted in a reverie perhaps, by someone who is not them, and not the viewer. They are being seen by an 'implied spectator', and we learn about the picture by coming to think through the perspective that the 'implied spectator' inhabits. We cannot be *in* the picture, we cannot own the figures in them. Instead we can attend to the conditions of their existence, the nature of their tensions, by doing hard work on the effects the implied spectator is having in the work of art that we are looking at (Wollheim 1987: 101–86).

In a wonderful section on Ingres, Wollheim raises the question as to whether the 'implied spectator' isn't in fact the artist's imagined self, a self that the artist dreams up as he sits and does his work, as he sits and paints. Wollheim suggests that the artist can only represent something, something that makes great art more than socio-historical, or exercises in pure painting, by finding 'secondary meaning' himself. The artist is himself watching his own creation, wishing for something that he does not understand, and when he manages it, the understanding of this achievement consists in seeing that the artist is himself being watched by his own dream, or mysterious wishes. Ingres, for example, fantasises in many of his finest works, an implacable, ideal father, one who will tolerate opposition without anger (as in the portrait of the banker Louis-François Bertin, 1833, in the Louvre) or give away his own wife to the son who has fallen in love with her (as in Ingres's recurrent interest in the story of Antiochus and Stratonice, from Plutarch's *Life of Demetrius*). What Wollheim is asking is that the observer of the painting sees the 'secondary meaning' that the artist has made by participating in the gaze of the 'implied spectator' who, as it were, sees and represents the real tensions of great paintings (Wollheim 1987: 277–8).

The reason for introducing these ideas from aesthetic theory is that they give a model for incorporating an aspect of male friendship that is not discussed enough, which is that part of our trust, and our interest in, our male friends comes in thinking about, and seeing them, engaged elsewhere (let us say with women) such that we always know them from some position that is not direct, not socio-historical or pure, but as it were mediated by our sense of their sexual destiny. In thinking about male friendship and the sexual vicissitudes that it exists to mitigate, we see our friends as we might see works of art: the struggles of their sexual existence force us into a rough and *engagé* version of connoisseurship. No direct access can be had; the nature of the friendship becomes a form of negotiation, a way of pondering the 'implied spectator', who is probably a lover, or a rival, or a composite figure from the sexual history that our friend has experienced. Friendship is a voyage around the Sphinx, or, as Ingres (and Freud) might prefer, a combined effort, by friends, to out-stare the returning gaze of false representation.

This can be put more directly, more pictorially. A notable effect (and the evidence for this may be historical and personal) of the orgy, the sexual orgy, is user-friendliness. Participation in sexual orgiastics does something that lonelier sexual activity does not allow. First, we can watch. Second, we don't feel left out, not because of any special sexual power that may have come upon us, but because we actually participate far more by not having to be omnipotent. Let us suppose we are in a flat in New York; our friends are hard at it elsewhere in the apartment. We go and make some tea; look out at the dawn light, coming up over the East River; we are both happy to be ordinary and naked, and also a participant who can observe and be observed. The essential feeling is that of friendship, because orgies strangely connect 'implied spectators' with democracy. More often than not, they are memorable and artful experiences. Why? The answer is that the experience of observing, of seeing the sexuality of male and female friends, is menacing only in the competitive imaginings generated by exclusion. Physical inclusion, of which the orgy is a fine example, generates ordinary feelings (our bodies seem both ordinary and desirable) and a complete lack of interest in omnipotence. Orgies give friendliness a chance, in the very place that is most supposed (in the Ciceronian ideal) to exclude them: sexuality. And the curious effect is the making explicit of the connection between watching, or looking at an idea of art, and democratic friendliness. The social history of the orgy can be said to contradict this hypothesis: in Imperial Rome, or at the court of Catherine of Russia, the orgy might be a trial of strength, or an arena of political menace and dehumanization. But the alternative view – the one I am proposing – must have equal force. By making one's admiration for the sexuality of others an unthreatening and palpable fact, shared experience of this kind permits sexual feeling to be included in friendship, by promoting two things that friendship cannot exist without: a perspective from which to admire, and a setting wherein the involvement of one's friend in deeply engrossing activity allows the fantasy of omnipotence to be dispelled (since the watching self, simply by being present, populates the space where the omnipotent self hoped to lord it alone). There is of course the objection (*à la* Eve Kosofsky Sedgwick) that in this example, male friends are simply once again showing off to each other. There is an infinite regress to this, however, and experience may be said to contradict it.

With a somewhat extravagant example, I have suggested that the experience of the sexual orgy is that of friendship, in this case between males. We observe our friends, and can make our friendship part of seeing the tasks upon which they are engaged as part of them. Some of this task will be sexual, some intellectual, some more routine. But the argument that male friendship is, in its deepest civic form, remote from feelings about sexuality is as exhausted as the argument that male friendship is, in the end, homosexual. Instead, and as part of the trust that friendship requires and inspires, a form of practical sexual admiration, free of the loneliness of omnipotence, could be said to be fundamental to authentic male friendship. We love to see our friends at work, blind to the actual beauty of what they do, in the same ways that we come to admire the depth of characterization in great portraits by seeing that they were not made for us. Our friends are not for us: they are for us in being at work themselves, without the need for the endless reiteration of love and devotion that the friendship of adolescence so disastrously insists upon. Some of what I've said is in Lawrence's *Women in Love*, and practically all of it in James Joyce's *Ulysses*. It is important that two great modern writers should be seen as bringing to the discussion of the roots of male friendship the admission of sexual senses that the classical humanist ideal so nobly attempts to do without.

And, as always, things go back to certain suggestions of Nietzsche. Once the lessons of the world have been drummed in, as Nietzsche sees them – once the pleasurable end of slave morality has come – a certain distant acknowledgment can be paid, between friends, who take on a kind of friendship of the future, emptied as they now are of the seriousness (and rivalries) of the past. They are, in Nietzsche's *The Gay Science*, aware of each other's merits; they know that the new journey has begun; they certainly (and this is part of Nietzsche's greatness as a philosopher of friendship) acknowledge each other's sexual force. They become what he calls 'star friends', locked in 'star friendship' (Nietzsche 1974: 225–6). They have met again, under different conditions, and inside ideals of respect quite remote from those of Christianity or Ciceronian humanism. They are lonelier, but no lonelier than modern man, who has made friendship either utilitarian or a half understood, pragmatic, act. They have admitted the need to negotiate certain dead forms together: they are 'like the stars' in Thom Gunn's fine reworking of the great, friendless Antony, in his 1961 Shakespearian poem, 'My Sad Captains' (Gunn 1979: 49).

> One by one they appear in
> the darkness: a few friends, and
> a few with historical
> names. How late they start to shine!
> but before they fade they stand
> perfectly embodied, all
>
> the past lapping them like a
> cloak of chaos. They were men
> who, I thought, lived only to
> renew the wasteful force they
> spent with each hot convulsion.
> They remind me, distant now.
>
> True, they are not at rest yet,
> but now that they are indeed
> apart, winnowed from failures,
> they withdraw to an orbit
> and turn with disinterested
> hard energy, like the stars.

REFERENCES

Cicero (1909) *De Amicitia* in *Offices* (Trans. T. Cockman and W. Welmoth), London: Everyman's Library, J.M. Dent & Sons Ltd.

Gunn, Thom (1979) *Selected Poems*, London: Faber.

Haughton, Hugh (ed.) (1988) *The Chatto Book of Nonsense Poetry*, London: Chatto & Windus.

Ignatieff, M. (1988) 'Lodged in the heart and memory', *Times Literary Supplement* April 15–21: 411–413.

Lamb, Charles (1985) *Selected Prose* (ed. A. Phillips), London: Penguin Books.

Miller, S. (1983) *Men and Friendship*, London: Gateway Books.
Nietzsche, F. (1974) *The Gay Science* (Trans. Walter Kaufman), New York: Vintage Books.
Richards, J. (1987) 'Passing the love of women', in J. A. Mangan and James Walvin (eds.) *Manliness and Morality*, Manchester: Manchester University Press.
Ricks, C. (ed.) (1987) *The New Oxford Book of Victorian Verse*, Oxford: Oxford University Press.
Sedgwick, E. K. (1985) *Between Men: English Literature and Male Homosocial Desire*, New York: Columbia University Press.
Wollheim, R. (1987) *Painting as an Art*, London: Thames and Hudson.

Chapter Five

FRIENDSHIP IN CHILDREN'S FICTION

MARGARET KINNELL

'Onth uponth a time' my two-year-old would lisp in imitation, as we obeyed the bedtime ritual, her encounters with stories beginning – as they did for her sister – in this nightly introduction to the terrors as well as the delights of 'three billy goats gruff' and company. All kinds of books in various stages of decomposition, were as much her necessary friends as the comfort blanket she lugged around so obsessively. In moments of stress there were problems of choice – a battered copy of *Mister Happy* or her ragged 'Qwoolt', with somewhere in the cot always the curled-up remains of a 'Ladybird' as back-up. Children don't so much learn *about* living through the reading of books: as Hoggart once described, reading becomes *like* living; even the most far-fetched of fairy tales, the most trite of cheap story-books are woven into the fabric of their everyday existence.

For today's child, meeting with good writers and illustrators like Helen Oxenbury or John Burningham is just as likely on the shopping trip to Sainsbury's as it is in library or bookshop. Post offices and newsagents all have their Ladybird displays at child-grab level; John Menzies' Early Learning Centres, which already stock children's picture books, are launching new 'stand-alone' children's bookshops, and parents are everywhere exhorted to encourage the leisure reading habit.

And with this wider availability comes a greater choice than ever before. Competition with other media has meant especially that leisure-sated children demand entertainment value from their reading. A child's viewpoint is today central to both theme and format, even in those books which still aim to *teach* children about life, as well as offering them vicarious living experiences through the act of reading.

Learning who your friends are, and what makes for friendship, are two of the more important of these lessons for childhood. Naturally, therefore, children's writers have frequently written on the issues surrounding these aspects of growing up, just as they have also felt it their business to proffer advice on all the other sides to children's behaviour, whether at work or play, in the home, at school, in factory, scullery or farmyard. But the crucial difference between modern and earlier children's fiction lies in the fact that many early writers clearly distrusted the idea that 'children know, instinctive taught, the friend and foe'.

Books for children have always underlined, and often with a heavy hand, what society expects for and from its progeny in their personal relationships; but until only recently in the two hundred and fifty year history of children's literature, books were usually written from an exclusively adult viewpoint. Children's books purveyed an adult view of friendship, just as they sold children a grown-up view of life in general. It is quite apparent that this eagerness to cozen children into an awareness of what makes people tick has resulted in far too much emphasis on adult preoccupations and values. The uncanny percipience of gifted young observers of morals and mores has been sadly underestimated. Even as a young girl, Jane Austen recognized that 'sensibility and feeling' provide a basis for only the most superficial of relationships: *Love and freindship* [sic] (written when she was fifteen) displays all of her later acuity, with heroines flying into each other's arms, young women who 'having exchanged vows of mutual friendship for the rest of our lives, instantly unfolded to each other the most inward secrets of our hearts' (Austen 1790: 107). Daisy Ashford's *The Young Visiters*[sic] demonstrates similar clear-sightedness on the part of a bright nine-year-old about the ways of adults in matters of love and friendship; no problems here for the child identifying what friendship is. A friend *does* things for you, even when you are 'not quite the right side of the blanket as they say', a friend may be counted on to advance your cause in the world whatever your origins (Ashford 1919: 45–6).

This presumption that adults hold the monopoly on insights into behaviour has a long tradition; early children's books were founded on the principle. Not only did writers concentrate on tedious explanations of how children should behave and what constituted suitable companions, they also made great play with first befriending the child reader – only then punching home the moral, usually with considerable certitude. John Locke, credited by the redoubtable Sarah Trimmer with providing much of the motivation behind the rise of the eighteenth-century children's book trade, introduced the idea that 'Fear and awe ought to give you the first power over their minds, and love and friendship in riper years to hold it' (Locke 1968: 146). The emphasis is all on controlling children's responses and moulding young minds.

Educating and carefully directing through befriending your pupil was a notion also popularized by Rousseau, that other influencer of early children's writers. Emile's tutor was to 'become a child himself, that he may be the companion of his pupil and win his confidence by sharing his games' (Rousseau 1911: 19). Authors took their role as children's friends both seriously and literally; the most celebrated popular example being Arnaud Berquin's *Ami des enfans,* published in English in 1783. Nothing was overlooked in his attempt to manipulate children into reading. According to Berquin, publishing *The children's friend* in monthly parts and in a pocket-sized format was a deliberate ploy 'by all the methods in his power, to interest them in his writings' (Berquin 1783: *x*). Having once caught your reader/friend then came the didactic tales on themes of selfishness, greed and lying – all those *adult* worries that suggested a rather less than amiable perspective on the eighteenth-century child reader. In his tale of 'The little fidler' [*sic*] Berquin's protagonists spend much of their time quarrelling and outdoing one another in charitable gifts to the poor musician, save for greedy Charles, much too busy stuffing cake into his mouth for acts of kindness. As in so many of these moralizing tales, the bad child is by far the most appealing and what we end up with is a neat vignette of the square peg, one who, as in all good didactic fiction, inevitably gets his come-uppance. While his 'friends' are praised for their charity, the independently cake-gorging Charles stands aloof and castigated, although surprisingly unbowed. The rather obvious lesson, that to be loved you must be generous to the unfortunate, is underpinned by an even more subtle and significant one: choose friends who disdain poor, begging fiddlers as much as you do. . . .

Following Berquin's example, authors were seemingly

determined on an amiable benevolence towards their readers. Eleanor Fenn's *Infant's friend* (1797) and Sarah Trimmer's *Servant's friend* (1787) were two popular examples, this latter somewhat chillingly 'designed to enforce the religious instructions given at Sunday and other charity schools, by pointing to the practical application of them in a state of service' (Trimmer 1787:*i*). Here too, 'healthful' companionship meant conforming to the prig's expectations, with swift retribution for those who persisted in pursuing the schoolboy pleasures of bird-nesting, play-ground mischief and the like. No doubt most of Trimmer's readers would rather snap back like idle Dick 'don't preach about it, I shall hear enough from my master' than be a friend to the appalling Thomas Simpkins, busying himself with 'hearty resolutions' (Trimmer 1787: 11–13).

Various editions of the original Berquin continued to be popular into the nineteenth century – they made excellent school prizes. A Scottish example was presented to Master George Scott of Leith in 1812, as 'a reward of merit' (Berquin 1798). There were also straight imitations: Mark Anthony Meilan's *The friend of youth* (1788) was especially prettily produced, with several neat engravings, although just as oppressively didactic. His bowdlerizing of 'The children in the wood' sets the tone of a book 'intended to excite attention, cherish feeling, and inculcate virtue'(Meilan 1788). A more lasting *Children's Friend* was the magazine which began in 1824 and continued publication, under different imprints, into the twentieth century. Its early editors included the Reverend William Carus Wilson, founder of Cowan Bridge School (the Lowood of *Jane Eyre*). What manner of friend he was to children can be judged from Charlotte Brontë's characterization of Mr Brocklehurst. His brother Charles, who edited *Children's Friend* between 1851 and 1854, was more likely in this role – 7ft 4in tall, he habitually lit his cigars at street lamps and was a well-known London character.

By 1909 the magazine had changed from its early evangelical fervour to a somewhat softer tone – despite sharing an imprint with two temperance journals, *The Band of Hope Review* and *The British Workman*. Its contents were a mix of competitions, letters, short stories and factual accounts of animals, travel and domestic trivia, all addressed directly, even somewhat conspiratorially, to the reader/friend:

> I wonder if you know anything about Japanese children, and
> will be interested to learn a few facts about them and their
> manner of living?. . . There are no buttons or hooks to be
> fastened up so I think it must be very easy for a Japanese child
> to dress – don't you?
>
> (*Children's Friend* 1910: 30)

Several of the most popular children's authors of the period also
wrote for the magazine. Dorothea Moore's 'The making of Ursula'
first appeared serially in July 1909, one of many tales that explored
boarding school friendships.

The demise of *Children's Friend* ended the last link with those
early children's tales that sought to befriend their readership out
of a grim determination to preach at them. Twentieth-century
children's writers would continue to see children as friends, even
addressing them in these terms on occasion, but without the moral
sting in the tail that always seemed to accompany those spurious
friendships offered by so many eighteenth- and nineteenth-
century authors.

Interestingly, children themselves did seem to feel that even
those first crude attempts at children's fiction had supplied the
kind of companionship that avid readers sought. Richard
Edgeworth, Charles Lamb and many others spoke affectionately of
John Newbery's children's books, books that broke new ground in
the mid-eighteenth century and which began the serious business
of English children's publishing and bookselling.

> When I was a child I had no resource, but Newbery's little
> books and Mrs Teachum.
>
> (Edgeworth 1814: 1)

Coleridge's son Hartley was even inspired to poetry in praise of his
favourite, *The history of little Goody Two Shoes*; and Charles Lamb
berated Mrs Barbauld, whose moralizing he felt had usurped
Newbery's pretty, dutch-gilded items.

For the solitary child, books were a welcome source of
companionship, perhaps the only sort available at times. To the
young Walter Scott, for example, they were both a delight and an
inspiration:

> . . .from the earliest period of my existence, ballads and other
> romantic poems I have read or heard as a favourite, and

sometimes as an exclusive gratification.

(Clark 1969: 49)

Wordsworth was similarly affected by his early encounters with fiction; although for him too it was the old tales he preferred:

> . . .the wishing cap of Fortunatus, and the invisible coat of
> Jack the Giant-killer, Robin Hood and Sabra in the forest with
> St George.

(Wordsworth 1979: 5 338–41)

From these very earliest attempts at a literature intended for children's pleasure readers responded eagerly to what was on offer: chap books, and later the more substantial children's books, were seized upon delightedly. Authors had no need to work at the business of relating to readers in the manner of Berquin. When writers and publishers eventually realized that children could be won over by the simple expedient of a good tale well told, then amusing fiction became more than a mere adjunct to the profitable school texts and moral tales. By the mid nineteenth century children's fiction stood on its own merits within publishers' lists.

For those children who were stirred to write for themselves following this early exposure to tale-telling, another dimension was added to the imaginative world unlocked by books. Creating your own fictions provided an even more satisfying pastime. Writing in 1839 at the age of twenty-three, Charlotte Brontë looked back over her childish fantasizing with a wistfulness that sprang from realizing that childhood was gone forever. Gone too were all those imaginary friends conjured to inhabit solitary moments: bidding farewell meant entering the unknown and strangely threatening world of adulthood:

> Yet do not urge me too fast reader: it is no easy theme to
> dismiss from my imagination the images which have filled it
> so long; they were my friends and my intimate acquaintances,
> and I could with little labour describe to you the faces, the
> voices, the actions of those who peopled my thoughts by day,
> and not seldom stole strangely even into my dreams by night.
> When I depart from these I feel almost as if I stood on the
> threshold of a home and were bidding farewell to its inmates.
> When I strive to conjure up new inmates I feel as if I had got

81

into a distant country where every face was unknown. . .

(Brontë 1986: 366)

Charlotte and Branwell's kingdom of Angria, and Anne and
Emily's Gondal, were the means of escaping a particularly grim
reality: after the deaths of their mother and two elder sisters, the
young Brontës lived a life of geographic and virtually total
emotional isolation in the Haworth parsonage. Charlotte's earliest
extant book, written when she was twelve, shows her need for the
warmth of a more conventional family, an urge to lose herself in a
compensatory world peopled by friends of her own creation.
Beginning 'There once was a little girl and her name was Ane'
[*sic*], she tells of a child who is taken to the seaside by two loving
parents and who cares for her sickly mother (Ratchford 1964: 18).
Unlike Jane Austen's early writings, however, intended as a passing
fancy to amuse the wider family circle, and then polished and
perfected to ensure a favourable reception, the Brontës' secretive
jottings confirmed them in their isolation. Charlotte's reliance on
imaginary friends made the realization of her limiting existence
even more painful.

The motivation behind Scott's first literary attempts was also
rather different from that of the young Brontës: like Jane, he had
a preference for sharing in the delight of yarning with *real* friends
– as a youth he and a companion would climb Arthur's Seat and
Salisbury Crags in Edinburgh, reading of knight-errantry and
imitating the tales with relish as they went:

> Sir Walter . . . used to recite for half an hour or more at a time
> . . . The stories . . . were interminable, for we were unwilling to
> have any of our favourite knights killed, and we copied such
> tales as we had read in Italian being a continued succession of
> battles and enchantments.

(Clark 1969: 122)

Writers for children who began their careers early were also
frequently influenced in this kind of way, either by close
friendships and family relationships that inspired them (the case
with the precocious Taylors of Ongar and with Lewis Carroll,
whose first magazines were composed when he was twelve to amuse
and tease his family), or by the need to create an intimacy that was
otherwise denied them as young writers. Beatrix Potter's *Journal*

reveals this desperate kind of loneliness; her invention of 'Esther', to whom she confided trivial incidents and amusing anecdotes, coincided with her finally doing what she'd found so difficult as a young child – getting the fruits of her imagination 'out' (Linder 1971: *xxv*; Linder 1966: 203–4).

Little wonder then that so much writing for and by children should be preoccupied one way and another with friends: first, through the initial motivation to write at all – either because a lack of sufficient companionship drove the child to its own imaging of friendship or, alternatively, as a way of sharing something secret and special with friends; secondly, in the themes of children's books and also, especially in the early days of publishing for children, through the marketing device of assuring children a form of surrogate, if authoritarian, friendship.

Beatrix Potter's writing for children displays some of these influences. Her books were first inspired by an intense empathy with the natural world, as in her creation of Esther, an interest that was partially a device to create some companionship. The writing of them only finally took shape through close friendship with the children of her old governess. It was this that inspired her most masterly of all accounts of animal/human relationships, *The Tale of Peter Rabbit*, whose cautionary theme, as with *Jemima Puddleduck*, is ironically to beware of falling into *un*friendly hands. Friendship, as well as the lack of it, had been a prime reason for Beatrix Potter getting started as a children's writer. It was not unnatural, therefore, that she should continue in a long tradition by making so much of it as a theme.

Avoiding, both metaphorically and in Peter's case quite literally, getting put in someone's pie or falling lackadaisically into the hands of a sandy-whiskered gentleman, has always been a concern in writing for children. Of all ideas about the nature of friendship in children's books this preoccupation with Hansel and Gretel figures is one of the earliest to appear as well as the most fundamental – knowing who can be trusted is after all essential for survival.

An early version of *The History of little Red Riding-hood* deals baldly with the issue:

> This story demonstrates that children discreet
> Should never confide in each stranger they meet

For often a Knave, in an artful disguise,
Will mark out an innocent prey for his prize;
Take warning, dear children, before 'tis too late
By little Red Riding-hood's tragical fate.
(*The history of little Red Riding-hood in verse* 1807: 14)

Being snatched by evil strangers was the most extreme danger to befall children who mistook friends: from the evidence of the numerous and truly horrific nineteenth-century stories of sweeps' apprentices spirited from their parents to a life of degradation, it seems this was a very real threat for children. Bogey-men, originally the stuff of folk and fairy tales, entered children's books in the guise of the master sweep, and have never left them.

But more subtle forms of false friendship posed equally serious threats, or at least so adults seemed to think. 'A fine mess you got me into' (or failed to help me out of) was another favourite story-line. The author of *Goody Two-shoes* (probably Goldsmith), wrote with feeling about the plight of the orphaned Margery and her brother Tommy, left to fend for themselves in the hedges and ditches, for 'Our relations and friends seldom take notice of us when we are poor; but as we grow rich they grow fond' (*The history of little Goody Two-shoes* 1766: 16). Awful warnings about the terrible consequences of mixing with companions who were 'wild and minded nothing but play' abounded. In *The entertaining history of Miss Lovegood and Miss Nogood, with that of Miss Tattle*, it seems unsurprising to a modern reader that Polly should prefer the company of the errant Nogood, 'that was in all manner of mischief, so that it was a scandal for any young lady to be seen in her company', to that of the dull if worthy and suitable Miss Kitty Thoroughgood (*The entertaining history* c.1780: 11). Yet the notion that children should have friends to uplift rather than tempt them into mischief was a strong feature of this early moralistic fiction. However unlikely that readers should be misguided enough to want such boringly perfect companions, authors seemed determined on presenting the ideal friendships between children as those in which spirituality, a high degree of mutual respect and a code of conduct fitted rather for Janeway's little saints than flesh and blood children, counted for more than good fellowship. In *Truth our best friend* Mary Elliott recounts a relationship between two boys that fails to meet these stringent criteria: one is weak and the other wilful, a morally fatal combination; neither is any good for the other — a friendship lacking in mutual respect inevitably, according to this code, becomes worthless and ultimately unhealthful, hence the priggish title (Elliott 1825).

An insistence on friendships serving a moral purpose was also to be found in the less obviously preachy novels of the later nineteenth century. *What Katy did*, published in 1872 and still, as one of the classics of children's fiction, read widely today, is largely concerned with Katy's growing awareness of real friendships and the bad effects of false ones. In the chapter on 'Intimate friends' Katy is impressed at first by the snobby Imogen, with her 'screwed-up, sentimental mouth, shiny brown hair, and a little round curl on each of her cheeks', but eventually has reluctantly to acknowledge the awfulness of a girl so totally wrapped up in herself. The contrast between Imogen and the saintly Cousin Helen, whose affection transforms Katy from wilful child to competent and considerate sister, points up the importance of good influences at key stages in an individual's development and how potentially disastrous unsuitable companions can be. And yet how wonderful the simpering Imogen, in her faded but still gloriously decadent party frock. The Imogens of one's childhood make it truly memorable, but these characters were played down by authors in favour of idealistic and therefore completely unlikely alternatives.

It would be good to think that younger authors have always confounded such deadening respectability, by writing in the same spirit as Jane Austen and Daisy Ashford — clear about their own judgement over what constituted suitability in friendship and unconcerned that adults' views might differ. Alice and Lucy's abortive friendship, in Austen's *Frederic and Elfrida*, provides a superb skit on adult perceptions. Alice's few small failings of drink, gambling and a filthy temper don't detract from her being seen by society as 'a most pleasing girl' (Austen 1793: 55–6). Her later study of truly dangerous friends — Mary and Henry Crawford's influence over *Mansfield Park* — is clearly anticipated in this novelette, written when Jane was only twelve. Puncturing the myth of adult infallibility on questions of personal relationships was an early skill, one that merely required honing to perfection for her later novels. Similarly, in her account of friendships which seem more fun than marriage, especially when marrying meant accepting an 'elderly' (forty-two-year-old) Salteena or a Helena Herring with 'very nice feet and plenty of money', Daisy Ashford set her face against convention. Ethel had the right idea. Better stay friends and wait for Another than take the wrong partner; no need to marry the man, even if he does get a title (Ashford 1919).

But few juvenile writers had either the wit or the genius of Austen and Ashford. Lucy Cameron, like her more famous sister Mary Sherwood a stout evangelical from the cradle, was as stern in youth as in her later writing. *The history of Margaret Whyte : or, the life and death of a good child,* which she wrote at seventeen, follows the progress of the heroine to her saintly death, a progress littered with the fruits of good works. Creating harmony amongst her friends appeared to be Margaret's single most important function in life, so that she died 'smiling upon her friends who stood round her', happy in the knowledge that she'd effectively preached the message that 'money and fine things can't make up for being thought ill of by one's friends' (Cameron 1827: 43–4, 66).

Friendship meant sweetness and light, trust and respect, all of the attributes that Mary Elliott also extolled. In *The sister's friend,* one of Lucy Cameron's many improving tales written as an adult, the same themes reappear: in this case harmony between sisters – each other's best friend – has to be safeguarded from the machinations of Miss Seaforth, unsuitably attractive, just like Coolidge's Imogen:

> Miss Seaforth possessed a certain smartness of manners which often passes with the inexperienced for real gentility, and which succeeded in exciting in her mind a considerable degree of admiration, and a feeling of something like awe.
>
> (Cameron 1831: 49)

Maria Edgeworth was similarly true to her later work in *The mental thermometer,* written when she was sixteen, an embarrassing tale about a young man's patronage by an older man, who as a mark of friendship bestows on the boy a handy thermometer for measuring the wearer's degree of 'happiness'; embarrassing not so much for its homo-erotic undertones as the gushing sentiment with which the narrator-hero expresses his admiration for the older friend, 'my second father, I may almost call him' (Edgeworth 1801: 380). While her later work lost the naïvety of this early effort, she continued to paint relationships in similarly glowing terms. Like

Rousseau, whom she and her father slavishly admired, Maria Edgeworth's writing contained a strong didactic element. Tale-telling, at which she excelled, was largely the means to a higher end, namely the inculcation of a rational and therefore totally unconvincing morality.

Depictions of friendship in children's fiction have, however, a lighter side. In addition to the commonplace tales that preached wariness of strangers, the avoidance of loose companions and how to make, and keep, suitable relationships, there have always been plentiful celebrations of comradeship and good fellowship in children's books. The mateyness of boys was recognized very early in the history of the literature – chapbooks of the eighteenth and early nineteenth century, even those with a clearly moral purpose, would make use of boys' delight in each other's company to condemn their nesting, truanting and apple-scrumping. 'Sir Gregory Greybeard' 's *Tommy and Billy, the brothers* and *The two boys and the bird's nest*, both published in pocket-sized format around 1792 to educate country children in a kind of early country code, also managed to describe recognizably average pals simply going out to have fun together. Thomas Day's *Sandford and Merton*, the most significant eighteenth-century book on the theme, similarly contrived to show Tommy Merton, spoiled son of a rich merchant, and local farmer's boy Harry Sandford enjoying an unlikely camaraderie, almost despite Day's tendentious moralizing.

The line leading straight from *Sandford and Merton* to William, Richmal Crompton's archetypal twentieth-century boy, also takes in a little-known study of nineteenth-century boyhood scrapes, written by the young William Martin, better known for his 'Peter Parley' tales. In *The hatchups of me and my school-fellows*, he offers the stories told to his school-fellows:

> after we had been sent to our dormitories; for we were put to bed as soon as it was dark, that we might be out of the way. . .
> I used to sit up in my bed and entertain my companions with various odd stories hatched up for the occasion.
>
> (Martin 1858: *v*)

In one of these, 'Robbing an orchard; or the parlour boarders', an adventure 'founded on truth', the four scrumpers – Winkle, Moffat, Pragen and Jenkins – have just the kind of awful luck that always seemed to befall the Outlaws; like them, they too lose neither their solidarity nor their joyous optimism – smashed cucumber frame, double-barrelled shotgun and guard dog on the loose notwithstanding. The peculiarly complex nature of these boy-boy friendships, in which companions in crime both compete in feats of derring-do and mutually support one another against a hostile adult world, began to be more fully explored in the increasingly realistic Victorian boys' school and adventure stories – first of all in Hughes' *Tom Brown's Schooldays*. Kipling's *Stalky and Co* was similarly based on his own school days and contains a great deal of mockery of earlier, less convincing accounts of schoolboy behaviour, in particular F. W. Farrar's *Eric, or little by little*. The tales of Ballantyne, Henty, Percy Westermann and others from the late Victorian and the Edwardian periods also contained plenty of examples of stout-hearted friends, but almost always of adolescent boys striving to be men. The first convincing, really popular exploration of small *boy* behaviour is to be found in the 'William' series, which had its origins in the less certain world between the two World Wars – although one of the central relationships, that between William and Ginger, appears to owe something to Bevis and Mark's friendship in Richard Jefferies' earlier *Bevis : the story of a boy* (1882). Unspoken acceptance of a common code is the key to William and Ginger, as indeed to all of the Outlaws' comradely sparring. To jostle and fight was all very well, but adult society was the common foe, and wringing the most out of every unlikely situation the agreed group objective. Turning the tables on life required co-operation between like-minded free spirits and, just occasionally, there were glorious moments of triumph that justified this co-operative effort.

Seeing their fathers scuppered in the very act of pinching the Outlaws' fireworks was especially rewarding; for they had betrayed the memory of their own childhood friendships in banning the boys' bonfire display. Sweet revenge then as Nemesis, in the shape of an outraged Colonel, set on by the Outlaws, proceeds to reclaim his property from the unsuspecting adults:

> The Outlaws followed. They walked brightly, expectantly, joyfully. Life was worth living, after all.
>
> (Crompton 1929: 190)

Such uninhibited joy at a successful skirmish in the long siege against adult supremacy is less often seen in girls' stories. School stories for girls, like those for boys, were some of the earliest means of exploring single sex relationships. One of the first, Mary Robson's *Rebellious schoolgirl*, set a tone that was followed in most succeeding accounts of boarding school life; much energy was expended in girls coping with the spite of their fellows, rather than uniting against adults, or indeed in simply enjoying life to the full. Girlish high jinks and 'crushes' were plentiful, but the theme of a heroine wrongly accused while a malicious school-fellow went free mopped up much of the action (Robson 1821). As with boys' stories more realism and less moralizing were offered in the stories of the late nineteenth and early twentieth centuries: Dorothea Moore, mentioned above, L. T. Meade and Angela Brazil helped popularize this sisterhood of the girls' school – a popularity still evident into the Fifties with the success of *The School Friend*. The 'Silent Three', the comic's principal 'firm chums', spent more of their time, though, in rescuing less capable females from distress than in realizing the potential of their alliance.

Nothing in fiction for girls matched the glorious joyousness of the Outlaws. Girl-boy friendships, perhaps understandably, have fared little better. In early tales it was uncommon, other than between brother and sister – and then usually because they'd been shipwrecked together – for mixed friendships to be a central theme. The most influential, Bernardin de Saint-Pierre's *Paul and Virginia* (1795), ended in death and disaster, and even here the couple were raised as siblings which made their 'mutual tenderness' somehow more acceptable.

Only modern children's books have really come to terms with the possibility of fully realized, non-sexual boy-girl friendships. Enid Blyton's 'Famous Five' and 'Secret Seven' series, while often ridiculed, did offer children their first easy read on this theme. Arthur Ransome's *Swallows and Amazons* broke new ground in exploring the dynamics of a mixed group, but it was Blyton who first provided children with a framework for their own imagining about boy-girl adventures. That Gene Kemp's *Turbulent term of Tyke Tiler* should make such an impact as late as 1977, through its celebration of equal opportunities in the school playground, shows how far we still must go. Child authors, somewhat surprisingly, have generally failed at exploring child friendships across genders. Daisy Ashford came close with her analysis of Ethel and Mr Salteena's relationship, but she was of course dealing with adults, not children, in *The Young Visiters*. Jane Austen too was never very interested in exploring friendships between children, of either sex. Adolescent girls' preoccupations were of greater concern to her. The Brontës' world was peopled by dukes, princes, statesmen and their ladies – not children. Inevitably those exceptional children who fictionalized were more concerned to fantasize about the adult world, or in Jane's case to develop her powers as observer and social commentator.

While children do indeed their friends 'instinctive know', adult writers have provided the essential perspective on childhood friends in children's fiction. Moralizing and warning of the dangers may have provided motivation for choosing the subject, but other factors soon took over – especially publishers' awareness of the changing educational philosophies that demanded a more winning approach to child readers. The significance of friends, or the lack of them, to the individual writer was a further influence. Goldsmith was acutely conscious of how much he owed to the kindly Newbery – the publisher who began it all: 'the philanthropic bookseller in St Paul's Churchyard, who has written so many books for children: he called himself their friend. . . .' (Darton 1982: 135).

Children's fiction could only begin through this initial commitment to the child as friend of writer and publisher, only develop for as long as the commitment continued. Today, children are eagerly wooed by publishers as never before. Friendship in children's fiction offers more than theme; it provides an organizing principle.

REFERENCES

Ashford, D. (1919) *The Young Visiters*, London: Chatto & Windus.

Austen, J. (1986) *The Juvenilia of Jane Austen and Charlotte Brontë* (ed. F. Beer), Harmondsworth: Penguin.

Berquin, A. (1783) *The Children's Friend*, Vol.1. London: T. Cadell and P. Elmsley.

——(1798) *The Children's Friend: a selection*, 3rd edn, Montrose: D. Buchanan.

Brontë C. (1986) *The Juvenilia of Jane Austen and Charlotte Brontë* (ed. F. Beer), Harmondsworth: Penguin.

Cameron, L.L. (1827) *The History of Margaret Whyte*, Wellington, Salop: F. Houlston and Son.

——(1831) *The Sister's Friend*, London: L.B. Seeley and Sons.

The Children's Friend Annual for 1910, London: S. W. Partridge and Co.

Clark, A. M. (1969) *Sir Walter Scott: the Formative Years*, Edinburgh and London: Blackwood.

Coolidge, S. (1872) *What Katy Did*, London: Blackie.

Crompton, R. (1929) *William*, London: George Newnes.

Darton, F. J. H. (1982) *Children's Books in England*, 3rd edn., Cambridge: Cambridge University Press.

Edgeworth, M. (1801) 'The mental thermometer', *The Juvenile Library* Vol.2: 378–84.

Elliott, M. B. (1825) *Truth our best Friend*, London: William Darton.

——(c. 1780) *The Entertaining History of Miss Lovegood and Miss Nogood, with that of Miss Tattle*, London: Robert Bassam.

——(1881) *The History of Little Goody Two-shoes*, London: Griffith and Farran (Facs. of 1766 edn.)

——(1807) *The History of Little Red Riding-hood in Verse*, London: B. Tabart.

Linder, L. (1966) *The Journal of Beatrix Potter*, London: F. Warne.

——(1971) *A History of the Writings of Beatrix Potter*, London: F. Warne.

Locke, J. (1968) 'Some thoughts concerning education', 5th edn. (1705) in J. L. Axtell, *The Educational Writings of John Locke*, Cambridge: Cambridge University Press.

Martin, W. (1858) *The Hatchups of Me and My School-fellows*, London: Darton and Co.

Meilan, M. A. (1788) *The Friend of Youth*, London: T. Hookham.

Ratchford, F. E. (1964) *The Brontës' Web of Childhood*, New York: Russell & Russell.

Robson, M. (1821) *The Rebellious School-girl*, London: Darton.

Rousseau, J. J. (1911) *Emile* (trans. B. Foxley), London: Dent.

School Friend Annual 1955, London: Amalgamated Press.

Trimmer, S. (1787) *The Servant's Friend*, London: T. Longman.

Wordsworth, W. (1979) *The Prelude 1799, 1805, 1850* (ed. J. Wordsworth), London: W. W. Norton.

Chapter Six

FRIENDSHIP AND PERSONAL DEVELOPMENT

ADRIAN FURNHAM

INTRODUCTION

Be courteous to all, but intimate with a few, and let those few be well tried before you give them your confidence. True friendship is a plant of slow growth, and must undergo and withstand the shock of adversity before it is entitled to the appellation.

George Washington

Do friends matter? What is a friend? How do the friendships we establish in early life affect our subsequent development? Does early friendlessness, for one or another reason, lead to later difficulties in establishing friendships in later life? Or is it possible that early deprivation from peers, some of whom may actually become friends, has its compensations? Indeed what is the function of early friendships? And does the nature of friendship change radically over the life span?

Clinical, developmental and social psychologists have pondered the above questions in their academic, and no doubt private, capacity for some time. Academic research into these issues has two interesting aspects. The first is that some have seriously questioned whether interrelated topics such as friendship, love and attraction merit serious (and expensive, in terms of time and money) research. For instance, the infamous Senator Proxmire from America who liberally handed out his *Golden Fleece* award 'for the biggest waste of taxpayer's money' gave such an award to a psychologist researching into love and attraction, on the grounds that some aspects of human nature should not be studied, and that ignorance is occasionally preferable to knowledge. Thus because friendship is so personal, so everyday and so different, research and findings would of necessity be soft, relying on retrospective self-report and unlikely to yield hard, generalizable, non-intuitive theories. Topics such as friendship formation – causes, consequences and effects – are thought by some to be best left to the domain of literature, popular speculation or social sciences less concerned with empirical rigours than with metaphysical speculation. Happily this latter school of thought has not prevailed, though academics researching in this area have not always received the respect they deserve from their peers.

The second aspect of research in this area is quite typical for psychologists. Many findings have focused on abnormal rather than normal patterns of behaviour, in the belief that failures of the behaviour pattern (the system; the mechanism) will most clearly inform one how it 'works' and what its functions are when operating normally. Hence psychologists tend to look at the experiences of the unemployed to inform them of the latent benefits of employment; they study depression to understand it as well as happiness; they seek out the brain-damaged to understand the normal functioning of the brain. Thus it has been argued that by looking at the friendless we see the functions and benefits of friendship; by looking at those people who find difficulty making any friends we get a clue to the characteristics of those who easily make friends. Whether this is indeed true is uncertain, but explains why psychological research appears so obsessed by the abnormal, the failed and the problematic, rather than the normal, the successful, the unproblematic.

The study of children's friendships has also been relatively ignored for another reason. Thanks mainly to psychoanalytic thinkers who stressed mother–child relationships as of paramount importance in child development, the child's friendships were seen as far less important, indeed themselves 'determined' by the parental relationship. That is, friendships were seen either as epiphenomenal, or else primarily determined by other things, such as personality, social class, parental attachment or even culture and geography. This rather simple-minded and dismissive view of friendship, however, no longer prevails and the study of friendship at all ages now merits serious theorizing and empirical investigation.

DO FRIENDS MATTER? THE FUNCTIONS OF FRIENDSHIP

But of all plagues good Heaven, thy wrath can send
Save me, oh, save me, from the candid friend.
George Canning (*New Morality*)

Even if psychologists do not, parents and teachers have known for a long time that children of all ages can provide particular resources for their friends that adults simply cannot. It has been argued by Rubin (1980) that children's friendships fulfil three major functions: first they teach children social skills which are necessary to establish, maintain and manage social interaction. Especially important among these are the ability to communicate and imagine oneself in the other person's role (empathize). Parents have become expert at interpreting and fulfilling the wishes of their children which may be expressed non-verbally, certainly inarticulately. Other children, however, are not as skilled, indeed they too are probably egocentric. Hence children have much to learn from each other about communicating their feelings and wants, and also about how to deal with conflict. Furthermore, families are hierarchical, whereas friendships are equal status relationships and it is important to learn to interact with peers, as well as superiors and subordinates.

Secondly, friendships provide a very useful means for social comparison. Children spend a great deal of time in friendships comparing tastes, skills, and abilities. These comparisons are necessary in the development of a valid sense of identity. By measuring themselves against others, children find out about their strengths and weaknesses, their abilities and limitations. This gives the child not only a good experience of the social reality of peers but also a clear sense of who they are.

Thirdly, children's friendships help the sense of group belonging. Children find an important sense of security in belonging to exclusive groups, and equally a sense of rejection if not part of a group. The experience of a socially supportive, mutually interested peer group is an important satisfaction available through peer friendships. But as Rubin (1980) points out, one should resist the temptation to romanticize children's friendships. Children's experiences and lessons learnt from peer friendships may also be undesirable. For instance, they may learn how to reject or stereotype peers, as well as how to engage in regressive and anti-social behaviour. That is, rather than enjoying trust, self-acceptance and shared values, children's early friendship patterns may cause insecurity, jealousy and resentment. Indeed they may learn the skills of self-deception most clearly. Thus the fact that friendships may be harmful only underlines their potential importance.

The major beneficial function of friendship is to teach the skills of friendship like the tactics of friendship-making (disclosing information, requesting information, extending friendships), and the skills of gaining entry to a group. But also children must learn how to be a friend – being attentive, approving and helpful.

Friendships therefore function to educate. Although few would take a completely naïve functionalist perspective, it is probably true to point out that friendships at all ages can fulfil various useful functions. The question therefore arises as to how those functions are fulfilled in the friendless.

THE CONSEQUENCES OF EARLY FRIENDLESSNESS

Every person, experiencing as he does his own solitariness and aloneness, longs for union with another.

Rollo May

For many years psychologists and educationalists have described various groups of rejected and neglected children and adolescents who seem to lack many of the appropriate skills that are to be important in both developing and maintaining peer friendships. It seems that poor social skills are associated with various interpersonal problems including friendlessness, and the converse, namely that good social skills and pleasant personality characteristics are associated with many friends and successful social, educational and occupational attainment. However, it is both naïve and misleading to assume a sort of 'simple determinism' where some early 'critical period', during which one can or cannot make friends, will necessarily predetermine the entire course of later development, including the ability to make friends. Nevertheless there are both empirical evidence and personal reports to suggest that early problems in establishing friendships are predictive of later problems of many kinds.

But if there is evidence of the deleterious effects of early friendlessness, how might the process operate? Social skills researchers (Trower, Bryant and Argyle 1978) have been careful to point out that it is difficult to untangle the causal directionality in studies of social skills. That is, for our purpose it cannot be said that lack of social skills causes friendlessness (and vice versa), or that friendlessness is the cause of lack of development in social skills. The two are bound up in a reciprocally causal relationship.

Despite this problem it may be possible to develop a model of the causes and consequences of friendlessness. Figure 1 proposes just such a model. The idea is quite simple: social incompetence or poor social skills may result from a variety of causes – poor mothering experiences, personality differences, an unenriching social environment. At any rate one would expect various consequences of being socially incompetent or inadequate. People who do not have many social skills tend not to make very good or interesting friends, and as both children and adults tend to be rejected and neglected; their resultant state of friendlessness and isolation is clearly not pleasant and these people may react in characteristically different ways.

Young adolescents may feel a sense of extreme anger at being unable to make friends, or at being neglected by significant and attractive others. They may turn to bullying those weaker but more socially skilled than themselves, aggressing against those who ignore or reject them, or performing acts of delinquency against property. Having no means (social skills) to achieve their desirable end (friendship), they attempt to humiliate those who have what they want.

On the other hand, some comfort themselves with food or drugs. This may be any substance popular or available at the time – glue, marijuana, alcohol etc. Rejected or shunned because of their egocentrism, lack of trust or unwillingness to share, some children, adolescents and adults cheer themselves up with food, or escape their immediate situation with stimulant (or depressant) drugs. Curiously, they may do this in small gangs which look like friendship cliques, but which have none of the qualities of real social groups. This cycle of behaviour has frequently been associated with depression in adults.

Finally, an easy way to escape a situation of rejection is fantasy. Some adolescents in particular encourage and indulge in escapist

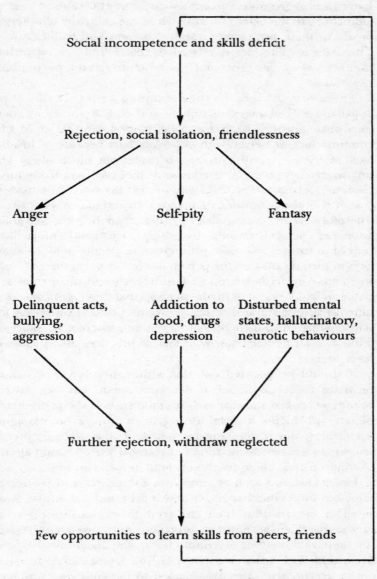

Figure 1 A measure model of the causes and consequences of friendlessness.

fantasies where they live in a world quite devoid of loneliness, hatred and aggression. This consistent fantasy may almost become 'addictive', to the extent that they shun the company of others in favour of their own private world of dreams and hallucinations. This state is quite clearly related to that found among various mental patient groups such as neurotics, and particularly psychotics.

The consequences of these 'coping styles' is of course maladaptive. The angry delinquent and bully becomes yet more unpopular and less likely to be befriended. The fat child who comforts him or herself with chocolate bars because of his/her lack of friends, confidants etc. becomes yet more obese and unattractive to potential friends and thus even less likely to be chosen as a friend. The child who prefers the world of fantasy to that of reality may be difficult to approach and hence is left alone. Therefore these 'coping styles', rather than helping the child, adolescent or adult establish friendships, are actually more likely to lead to further rejection, withdrawal, neglection and isolation. This in turn means that the person has few opportunities to learn the skills of friendship, and hence the whole process is perpetuated. Worse, this model suggests that things get worse over time, as people spiral downwards from a position of having few skills compared to their peers to a position where their skills are fixed or even reduced (through lack of practice), while those of their peers increase.

It should be pointed out that although this is a dynamic, recursive feedback model, it does not mean that this pattern cannot be broken and that early friendlessness is always predictive of later problems in establishing, maintaining or managing friendships. But it does suggest how and why there frequently appears to be some association between early friendship patterns of children and subsequent adjustment in social groups.

However, terms such as attraction, acceptance and friendship are often used interchangeably in this area, but it is unwise to do so. The factors that lead children to become popular or unpopular, that is accepted by the group or not, are not necessarily the same as those that determine the quality, quantity or type of friendship. For instance Hartup (1975) found children's peer group acceptance statistically related to the following variables: sociability, co-operation, friendlessness, self-esteem, empathy, low anxiety, intelligence, academic achievement, birth-order, their first name, sex and ethnicity. Children high in these factors are high in peer status, and tend to do well academically and become socially skilled. But a child's level of peer group acceptance does not necessarily relate to his or her personal intimacy with other children or his/her capacity to form and maintain friendships.

That is, to reinforce the point about the lack of determinism, the different factors coming into play in being accepted and establishing friendships, which mean early rejection or acceptance, do not necessarily lead to later rejection, or acceptance by others as a friend.

WHAT IS A FRIEND?

Your friend is the man who knows all about you, and still likes you.
E. Hubbard

Just as with adults, children and adolescents have many definitions of, or criteria for describing their friends. A great insight into the child's world of friendship can be gained by asking them simple questions, like what sort of people make good friends, how does one get a friend and what does it mean to be a friend.

Young children see their own desires and preferences as a sufficient basis for friendship nomination. As children get older they tend to emphasize less physical attributes and concentrate on psychological compatibility in interests, values, and outlook. Similarly, young children tend to believe friendships are formed by simple acts like playing or disclosing one's name. They tend to understand friendships in terms of momentary, physical interaction, but as they get older they tend to perceive the gradual developmental process that is actually involved in friendship formation. It takes some time for children to move from a view of friendship as being momentary and physical to it as being mutual sharing intimacy.

Relatively little is known as to what children expect from their friends, how these expectations change over time and the impact of their beliefs on friendship choice. Most child and developmental psychologists have pointed out that it is dangerous and misleading to generalize about friendship from adults to children or adolescents. Because of the vast and dramatic cognitive, physical and emotional changes that occur, it seems that there is probably a developmental path that children follow in the way in which they choose and lose friends as well as the way in which they actually conceive of the process.

Despite inherent problems with all stage-wise models, some attempts have been made to specify a developmental scale. Bigelow and La Gaipa (1980) have suggested that children aged 6–15 years pass through three major phases in their understanding of friendship. In the first phase (the situational phase), shared common activities, propinquity and simple evaluations seem the major determinants of friendship formation. In the second phase (the contractual phase) it is mainly character admiration. However, it is not until the third phase (the internal-psychological stage) that ideas of loyalty, commitment, mutual acceptance, genuineness and intimacy appear.

Others have come up with rather different but overlapping phases. For instance Selman and Jaquette (1977) described five: (i) momentary physical playmate; (ii) one-way acceptance; (iii) fair weather co-operation; (iv) intimate, mutual sharing; (v) autonomous interdependence.

One interesting observation from the work on child as well as adult friendship is the parallel between children's relationship growth (with increasing age) and adults' relationship growth (over short periods of time). Duck *et al.* (1980) have speculated on this point thus:

> What is lacking is a statement of the conceptual similarities and differences in the qualitative nature of *adults'* and *children's* personal friendships. We believe there are many similarities which are not confined to those that are manifested by the parallel ways in which researchers have dealt with the two topics. For example, if one attends to the factors which have been shown to influence adult relationship growth then there is a marked parallelism between the way in which adult acquaintances develop with time and the basis on which children form their relationships at different ages: both start with the influence of the objective characteristics of the partner (like physical attractiveness, status); are subsequently

influenced by behavioural style (e.g. non-verbal activity, level of aggressiveness); become centred on the understanding of motives behind the observed behaviour (e.g. by means of attribution or role taking): and ultimately focus on the character that lies behind the motives (e.g. trait description or comprehension of another's personality characteristics).

Adult acquainting may be conceived to be a communicative process with the ultimate aims of obtaining the maximum amount of information about the detail of the partner's personality (notably about his person constructs). Adult acquainting, in this view, is motivated by a search for support for one's own 'personality' provided in the form of similarity in most cases. The progress of adult relationships is restricted by the limits imposed upon what one *can* know about another person after given lengths of time spent acquainting, by a need for context in order to make useful inferences about the partner's personality and so on. Clearly in the case of children the limits are going to derive from the child's imperfect skills in social interaction: before the child can employ the crucial kind of search for personality detail that is essential to successful adult acquainting, s/he must be able to appreciate what s/he discovers and must therefore have developed the ability to interpret another person's behaviour in relevant terms. In the case of children's friendships then, our analysis must concentrate on how these skills develop if we are to elucidate the parallelism between children's and adults' acquainting. In children the acquaintance sequence is complicated (and limited) by the fact that children are learning in many different areas of 'cognitive' and 'social' competence at the same time as they are learning to interpret, and themselves produce, the behaviours that are implied by a given stage of relationship development.

(Duck *et al.* 1980: 90)

Rubin (1980) has suggested that these developmental stages move along the dimension of social understanding: (i) The ability to take other people's points of view – children have to move from the one-sided, egocentric view in which a friend is defined exclusively in terms of what he or she can do for one, to the perspective of the third-person who appreciates interlocking needs and provisions. The ability to empathize is a measure both of cognitive *and* social maturity.

(ii) The movement from seeing people as physical entities to seeing them as psychological entities. This is the shift from perceiving friends in physical, behavioural, concrete terms to the use of abstract psychological concepts. The quality and quantity of psychological appraisals of one's friends may also be seen as an important developmental measure.

(iii) The development of a time perspective, seeing friendships as enduring over time rather than as fixed in the here and now. This is the development of the concept of friendship in terms not of encounters but in terms of relationships.

Children then, in the thinking about and experiencing of friendships, move from focusing on the concrete to the abstract, from the immediate and observable to the inferred psychological characteristics of people. Given that they tend to pass through these various developmental phases, it may be possible to detect whether children and adolescents are advanced or retarded for their age in their friendships.

CHOOSING FRIENDS

Money can't buy friends, but you get a better class of enemy.

Spike Milligan

Under what circumstances do two comparative strangers who meet develop a liking for each other? What factors lead children, adolescents or adults to develop friendship with some people but not others? Researchers interested in this issue have listed a number of factors which are not meant to be thought of as exclusive. Indeed all might be necessary and it is doubtful if any are sufficient.

Physical proximity or propinquity

It has been said that when you are not near the one you love, you love the one you are near. Many studies have examined friendship patterns of people in large institutions like schools, universities, the military and found the factor most likely to determine resulting patterns of friendship was simple physical space – the closer you were the more likely you saw people, got to know them and befriend them. A charming study by Segal (1974) showed how police recruits were assigned seat and dormitory space alphabetically in terms of their surnames. After six weeks of training they were asked to nominate their three closest friends. The findings showed that the closer together the first initials of their last names, the more likely it was for them to become friends. No doubt that is why people marry the boy or girl next door – the closer the proximity, the more one interacts and the more friendly people get.

Familiarity

Does familiarity breed contempt or friendship? There is considerably less evidence of the former and more of the latter. Liking for people, and indeed inanimate objects, has been shown to be positively correlated with how often they are seen. Zajonc (1968) has talked of the mere exposure effect which suggests that irrespective of people's initial reactions to others or objects, they will get to like them more, the more they are exposed to them.

Parisians' attitudes to the Eiffel Tower moved from contempt to admiration, and audiences' reactions to Stravinsky's *Rite of Spring*, which first saw exits *en masse* but now is greatly admired, are examples of this phenomenon. Certainly the results suggest that the more children, adolescents and adults see of each other, and become familiar with each other's appearance, mannerisms and personality, the more likely they are to befriend one another.

Similarity

Do opposites attract or do birds of a feather flock together? There is in fact now abundant evidence that people who share common attitudes, interest and values are more likely to be attracted to each other and establish a friendship. In fact it has been suggested that one can actually establish a law of attraction which shows that attraction to others (and therefore the likelihood of establishing friendship) is a positive linear function of the proportion of similar attitudes. Indeed this is how computer dating services work, by attempting to match people's interests. In fact research projects have put people together with similar and dissimilar attitudes and shown how the former are much more likely to establish friendships than the latter (Byrne, Erwin and Lamberth 1970).

Complementarity

Some people have suggested that when the dispositions of one person (to be dominant, nurturing or talkative) fulfil the needs of another (dominated, nurtured and quiet) they will be attracted and establish friendships. The friendship of Laurel and Hardy exemplifies this idea. Research findings are not as clear cut here – there is evidence that people with aggressive needs tend to form friendships with people who have abasement needs but it may be that some dissimilar needs are complementary and others not; as yet it is unclear which are which.

Rewardingness

Put most simply, we like those who reward us most frequently and for that which we value and enjoy, while turning away from those who either do not reinforce us enough for the things we value, or do not do so spontaneously. This commonsensical notion has much going for it, particularly when it comes to children.

Friends provide tangible concrete rewards like money, advice, presents, but also social rewards, particularly support in difficult times. This reward is usually returned in the form of representing and hence one sees the development of a mutually interdependent and friendly relationship.

What are the antecedents of friendship? Studies have revealed the following list, which is not presented in rank order, and which describes various, probably related, features of people which make them attractive and hence likely to become a friend.

1. If the person has similar attitudes, beliefs, values, behavioural preferences and personality traits.
2. If the person satisfies, rather than ignores or frustrates our needs.
3. If the person is physically attractive.
4. If the person is socially competent.
5. If the person is generally pleasant and agreeable to us and our associates.

6. If the person reciprocates our liking.
7. If the person is generally in geographic proximity.

Clearly this list of factors is taken from studies on adolescents and adults. Young children, as has been noted, use different and more simple criteria for friendship. The above list is probably not exhaustive, nor is it culture-free. It may also be time-bound. That is to say, precisely which of the above factors are the primary determinants of friendship choice may differ, depending on a person's individual needs and personality, the culture and sub-culture from which they come and the particular period in time being considered. Nevertheless it does seem that some reasonable predictions can be made as to whether strangers who meet for the first time are likely to establish a friendship.

THE BASES OF FRIENDSHIP

I have always differentiated between two types of friends: those who want proofs of friendship, and those who do not. One kind love me for myself, and the others for themselves. Both are right, but I am not wrong.

Gerard de Nerval

Once people have met each other and become attracted, what determines whether they shall become and stay friends? Predictably there are quite different theories which have focused on quite different aspects of relationship. *Reinforcement theory* suggests that we like people who reward us, the greater the quantity, quality and frequency of reward (of whatever type), the more the liking and the stronger the friendship. This old-fashioned, but nonetheless quite plausible approach suggests a benign cycle of events – rewards induce liking and early friendship, liking leads to expectations of rewards which in turn encourage further interaction; if further rewards are obtained, further increments in attraction and depth of friendship are probable. Of course the issue is complicated by the sheer number of types of reinforcement which may be given, so that one may strongly reinforce one behaviour, ignore another and punish a third. Similarly it is not certain if strongly reinforcing or rewarding one need is equivalent to, or better than, moderately rewarding two needs. Nevertheless there is clear mileage in the theory which may be profitably taught to children and adolescents, particularly those who find friendships puzzling and problematic. *Exchange theory* is derived from economics, and hence stresses costs and benefits. The idea, quite simply, is that in exchange with others if benefits exceed costs we will continue friendships, but if costs exceed benefits those friendships will terminate. Put succinctly, the theory argues that people are rational and hedonistic, and base their friendship decisions on the probability and value of outcomes; in the pursuit of reinforcements people attempt to maximize their rewards and minimize their costs; and people are interdependent for their outcomes and thus must exchange rewards to obtain them. Of course these concepts help explain why people leave relationships – if a present friendship provides less 'profit' than a person could expect from someone else, that person will terminate it, yet people do remain 'loyal' in highly unrewarding relationships, presumably because they believe they could not do better. Similarly the more possible alternatives a person has, the more control he or she has in any particular relationship. *Gain-loss theory* refers to the observation that people like someone more who provides strokes sparingly and with discrimination. That is, neither someone who is hard to please, nor someone who always gives praise, is considered as attractive as people who give varied, honest feedback. But of course we get all sorts of feedback from different people about the same event, even occasionally at the same time and it becomes rather difficult to know which we pay attention to or why.

Depth theory views all friendship as a developmental process where two people engage in give-and-take and disclosure of personal information. It is particularly the latter display of trust which induces reciprocal disclosures and the possibility of a deeper relationship. In a sense this is not a theory in the way the above are theories, but a description of the phases one goes through in friendship.

There are a number of interesting ideas which may emerge from the morass of theory and research. The first is the concept of an *optimal amount* of some quality or process. That is, both too many and too few acts of friendship, such as self-disclosure of information, gift-giving, social support, are considered inappropriate. There is no linear relationship between the exchange of a quality and the establishment and maintenance of a friendship. Getting it 'just right', that is optimizing the ideal amount of a behaviour, is thus important in friendship.

The second concept is that of *reciprocity* of various qualities like information, material goods, emotional support. Where the reciprocity is not felt equal, just, or fair, the friendship is likely to dissolve. However, it should be pointed out that reciprocity does not necessarily involve kind with kind, but a reciprocity of different qualities in some sense equal in value.

Thirdly, all the theories suggest a *multiplicity of criteria* that are shared, considered important and reciprocated in a friendship. That is, people give and get a wide range of benefits while in a friendship, and it is possible that people give and get quite different things yet are extremely happy in the relationship.

To some extent observers might find all of the above theories callous, computational, economic models of a psychological process, that have no room for selflessness, altruism or non-reciprocated friendship. For many the essence of the process is not economic, nor rational. Indeed psychoanalytic interpretations might even argue that friendship choice is not even determined by conscious factors.

ARE THERE 'FRIENDLY TYPES', OR IDEAL FRIENDLY SITUATIONS?

Purchase not friends by gifts, when thou ceasest to give, such will cease to love.

Thomas Fuller

At the very heart of a great deal of controversy in nearly all the social sciences is the extent to which certain behaviours or personality traits are determined by internal, genetic or biological factors, or external, situational or environmental factors. The arguments become most passionate about such issues as intelligence or sex differences. But what about the ability to, or need to, make friends (at all ages). Are there personality types who seek out or shun friends?

There is some evidence to suggest that to some extent one can talk about 'joiners' and 'loners'. Joiners, people who need people, tend to have high affiliative needs. People with high, as opposed to

107

low, affiliative needs tend to be particularly concerned with establishing, maintaining and restoring positive friendships, with joining clubs, carefully observing others and communicating with them in a friendly way. Yet those highly affiliative, particularly friendly types, tend to fear rejection by others, they tend to avoid making derisive or offending comments, and tend to have high levels of anxiety in social settings. This anxiety over being accepted and not giving others negative (and perhaps honest) feedback means that although those with high affiliative needs seek friends constantly, they may not themselves make very satisfactory friends.

At the other end of the scale are loners who either choose to avoid others, preferring isolation, or find it difficult to make friends. Although there are introverted people who seem relatively happy with their own company and do not enjoy befriending others, the vast majority of comparatively friendless people appear to be so because they are shy, feel intensely awkward in social situations, experience considerable self-doubt and are even socially 'phobic'. There are, of course, both different causes of loneliness and different reactions but an important distinction is between *trait* loneliness and *state* loneliness. The former is a stable pattern of feeling lonely, which changes little over time or from situation to situation. On the other hand, state loneliness is a more temporary experience, often caused by some dramatic change in one's life.

If there is evidence of friendly and unfriendly types, is there evidence of friendly and unfriendly situations? That is, are there situations that promote friendship formation and others that inhibit it? Argyle *et al.* (1981) have argued that where people from homogeneous backgrounds come together and take part in a shared social activity, in a pleasant environment where social rules and conventions emphasize polite, open exchange, people tend to initiate friendships. Encounter and T- groups attempt to short-circuit friendship and familiarity, usually by playing special games or doing tasks that create physical contact and self-disclosure. After initial tension, people often begin to relax and if they have had to introduce themselves and reveal certain information about themselves, this may provide a basis for further conversation or a sense of group feeling.

Conversely, of course, there may be situations which inhibit friendship formation. The idea of person types and situation types that might help or hinder friendship leads on to the well-established idea of a *fit* or complementarity between persons and situations, such that a sagacious and astute combination of the two leads to the maximum (or minimum) probability of friendships being established.

CONCLUSION

Has psychological research enriched or obfuscated our understanding of friendship? Do psychological concepts and jargon clarify the complicated and subtle processes involved in friendship formation or render this common occurrence more obscure?

It is difficult to take sides in answering the above questions. But social science research into everyday processes like friendship is bound to be confronted with two problems – discovering what is well-known, commonsensical, matter-of-fact, and hence somewhat of a waste of time; and secondly the problem of the sloppiness, lack of rigour and ambiguity of everyday language and terms referring to friendship and the consequent necessity to develop a new jargon. The first is more apparent when counter-intuitive findings are revealed – the idea that physical attractiveness is not the most important determinant of attraction or that friendship is really only about the economic exchange of psychological commodities – they may be rejected precisely because they are counter-intuitive. Hence researchers are trapped, because if their results are intuitively understood, they are thought of as a waste of time, but if counter-intuitive, wrong. Similarly, using everyday language limits precision, so specific terms are used which may be seen as jargoning attempts to make the everyday and obvious inaccessible. But if the terms are correctly understood and used, they provide researchers with a clear language in which to communicate their findings.

Whatever the source of information – experience or scientific research – there seems evidence that the quality and quantity of friendships have very important psychological consequences. Furthermore, just as individual friendships show a clear developmental pattern, so does the business of learning how to become friends develop over the life span. Most importantly, because a state of friendlessness has nearly always been associated with distress, and because people have to learn how to master the subtleties and difficulties of friendship formation, a person's earliest real friendships may have crucial consequences on their later development.

REFERENCES

Argyle, M., Furnham, A., and Graham, J. (1981) *Social Situations,* Cambridge: Cambridge University Press.

Bigelow, B. and La Gaipa, J. (1980) 'The development of friendship values and choice' in H. Foot, A. Chapman and J. Smith (eds) *Friendship and Social Relations in Children,* Chichester: John Wiley.

Byrne, D., Erwin, C., and Lamberth, J. (1970) 'Continuity between the experimental study of attraction and real-life computer dating', *Journal of Personality and Social Psychology* 16: 157–65.

Duck, S., Miell, D., and Gaebler, H. (1980) 'Attraction and communication in children's interactions', in H. Foot, A. Chapman and J. Smith (eds) *Friendship and Social Relations in Children,* Chichester: John Wiley.

Hartup, W. (1975) 'The origins of friendship', in M. Lewis and L. Rosenblum (eds) *Friendship and Peer Relations,* New York: Wiley.

Rubin, Z. (1980) *Children's Friendships,* Glasgow: Fontana.

Segal, M. (1974) 'Alphabet and attraction: an unobtrusive measure of the effect of propinquity in a field setting', *Journal of Personality and Social Psychology* 30: 654–7.

Selman, R. and Jaquette, D. (1977) 'Stability and oscillation in interpersonal awareness: a clinical-developmental analysis', in C. Keasey (ed.) *The Nebraska Symposium on Motivation,* Lincoln: University of Nebraska Press.

Trower, P., Bryant, B., and Argyle, M. (1978) *Social Skills and Mental Health,* London: Methuen.

Zajonc, R. (1968) 'Attitudinal effects of more exposure', *Journal of Personality and Social Psychology* 9: 1–27.

Chapter Seven

HUMANS, ANIMALS, AND THE LIMITS OF FRIENDSHIP

JAMES SERPELL

INTRODUCTION

In 1808 the poet Byron composed an inscription for the tomb of a dead friend, which ended with the following verse:

> Ye! Who perchance behold this simple urn
> Pass on – it honours none you wish to mourn.
> To mark a friend's remains these stones arise;
> I never knew but one, – and here he lies.

The friend in question was a Newfoundland dog called Boatswain.

In Byron's day such affectionate sentiments were only rarely applied to animals. Domestic animals were regarded primarily as servants rather than friends, and they were expected to earn their keep. Indeed, in the same year, when Richard Martin MP attempted to introduce a bill outlawing cruelty to animals, he was literally laughed out of Parliament (Singer 1983). Attitudes, however, were changing. By the end of the Victorian era a considerable body of legislation protecting animals had been enacted in Britain, and it had become relatively commonplace and respectable to refer to pet animals – dogs, cats and, to a lesser degree, horses – as friends, or even as best friends (Ritvo 1987). The trend has continued to the present day. At the moment, roughly half the households in northern Europe and North America contain pets, and the results of surveys in Britain, the United States and elsewhere confirm that the principal motive for keeping such animals is the provision of 'friendship' or 'companionship' (Mugford 1980; Serpell 1986). The friendship role of pet animals is now so widely acknowledged in the relevant literature that the word 'pet' – regarded by some as mildly derogatory – is being gradually replaced by the term 'companion animal'.

Despite this historical change in perceptions of animals, and popular adherence to the view that dogs and other pets make excellent friends, the concept of friendship continues to be applied relatively exclusively to human relationships. Although non-human animals are commonly said to engage in friendly interactions, the words 'friend' and 'friendship' are rarely used in studies of animal social relationships, and the general impression created is that animals do not form friendships with each other, at least not in the sense that humans do. All of this raises some interesting questions about the nature of friendship. Is friendship, for example, a uniquely human innovation and, if so, why? Or do comparable relationships bearing different labels exist in non-human species? Conversely, if animals do not form friendships, in what sense can a dog (or horse, or any animal) be seriously regarded as man's best friend?

TOWARDS A DEFINITION OF FRIENDSHIP

Before tackling the issue of whether or not animals form friendships with each other, it is necessary to propose a formal description of human friendship which takes into account not only its typical structure but also its putative functions. In practice, this is no easy task, since friendship is, at best, poorly defined and it often means different things to different individuals. The term, for instance, has been used to describe 'momentary physical playmates' among young children between the ages of roughly three and five years, although most authorities would agree that children of this age are too egocentric to grasp the complexities of adult friendship. By the age of eleven or twelve, children's conceptions of friendship approach closer to the adult pattern. Friendships are seen as enduring relationships which develop over a period of time, and friends are viewed as sources of intimacy and support. Older children are also aware of the importance of psychological compatibility between friends, comprising such things as shared interests and mutually agreeable personality characteristics (Rubin 1980). But even at this age and older, individual concepts of friendship vary considerably from person to person. It is also far from clear whether the term friendship, as it is understood in the modern West, necessarily has equivalents in other cultures (see Alexander 1979). With these caveats in mind, however, it is nevertheless possible to identify features that characterize most so-called 'friendships', and which at least partially distinguish them from other kinds of social relationship.

First, friendships are traditionally non-sexual relationships. This statement should not be taken to imply that sex and friendship are incompatible, but rather that it is possible for two individuals to engage in a sexual relationship without necessarily being friends, and vice versa. In other words, the underlying motivations are fundamentally different. The results of various studies also suggest that people form the majority of their friendships with members of the same sex as themselves (Kimmel 1979). Secondly, friends tend to be non-relatives. Again, this does not mean that it is impossible to have a relative as a friend. It is simply that in practice the two categories of relationship are generally classified as separate. Thus relatives are usually referred to in terms of kinship – my father, my nephew, my cousin, my daughter – while friends are simply friends. It is also possible actively to dislike and avoid a relative, whereas a friend would cease to be classified as such if this were the case. This fact emphasizes the element of choice in friendships. Individuals choose their friends, but they are stuck with their relatives, whether they like them or not. It should be emphasized, however, that these rules are less apparent in other societies. In some cultures, for example, kinship terms such as 'brother' or 'uncle' are also used to describe non-relatives (Alexander 1979). Thirdly, friendships tend to be relatively egalitarian, reciprocal relationships involving individuals of similar age and social status. There are, of course, numerous exceptions to this rule but, in general, people tend to select their friends from those within the peer group with whom they are on terms of reasonable equality.

Friendships can also be described in various ways: in terms of the kinds of interactions friends engage in, how these interactions are distributed, the overall quality of the relationship, and a number of other parameters, such as intimacy, reciprocity, complementarity, interpersonal perception and commitment (see Hinde 1979). Regarding the sorts of things friends do together – i.e. the content and diversity of their interactions – friendships are clearly highly variable, although certain generalities emerge.

113

Friends, for instance, tend to spend relatively large amounts of time in close proximity. Of course, some friends may not have seen each other for years and may only exchange Christmas cards, but such long-distance friendships are generally based on closer associations at some time in the past. Friends also tend to engage in a wide range of different activities together, although it is nearly impossible to specify the types of activities, beyond saying that friends tend to share similar or compatible interests. In this respect, there is some evidence of a sex difference in friendship; men, on the whole, emphasize the importance of shared interests and activities, while women tend to stress the role of affect and reciprocity (Kimmel 1979). The provision of mutual support and aid is undoubtedly also a crucial element of friendship, hence the old adage that 'a friend in need is a friend indeed'. Despite this, a study of middle-class American women found that people received less help, overall, from their friends than from their relatives. Exchanges of helping interactions within friendships are also carefully balanced. Whereas people seem content to receive help from their kin without necessarily reciprocating, they are reluctant to become too indebted to their friends (Essock-Vitale and McGuire 1985). Indeed, persons who become overly dependent on the aid of friends tend to be perceived as a burden.

In terms of the relative frequency and patterning of their interactions, friends tend to mesh well with each other. We select our friends not only on the basis of general similarities, but also on their ability to fit our particular needs for social interaction.

Ideally, the quality of relationships between friends is positive, warm and mutually rewarding. Friendships are rarely entirely free of conflict, but the relationship will tend to disintegrate if conflicts become serious or insoluble. Many friendships also involve a competitive element, although competition within friendships is generally playful rather than serious.

Both short- and long-term reciprocity are characteristic of friendly interactions. Friends who forget to answer letters or phone calls, or who consistently fail to return dinner invitations or favours, tend not to remain friends, unless they are already very old and trusted. This 'you-scratch-my-back, I'll-scratch-yours' element is especially important during the early stages of friendship formation, and it is also essential that any sense of obligation or indebtedness does not become too one-sided. Complementarity

114

may also be important in many friendships. For example, a power-motivated individual might seek friendships with weaker subordinates, and vice versa. People may also like one another because somehow they bring out the best in each other, irrespective of whether or not they share similar attitudes or interests.

The degree of intimacy in friendships depends to a large extent on the individual propensities of those involved, although idealistic conceptions of friendship place strong emphasis on intimacy, at least at the level of mutual self-disclosure. Intimacy in friendships is therefore inextricably bound up with mutual trust, since people are understandably reluctant to reveal themselves to individuals who cannot safely be entrusted with confidences. Friends need to be tolerant as well as trustworthy. They are expected to accept us as we are without serious criticism, even if what we reveal about ourselves is not entirely to their liking. Together, intimacy and mutual trust are commonly used as criteria for judging the closeness of friendships. Our closest or best friends tend to be those whom we trust implicitly, and to whom we consequently reveal most of ourselves (Altman and Taylor 1973). Although it often exists, physical intimacy is not a necessary ingredient of friendship. Indeed, in some Western societies it may be actively avoided, particularly among male friends.

As far as interpersonal perception is concerned, friends on the whole tend to score higher than relatives. We like to believe that our friends understand our true personalities, and may even know us better than we know ourselves. In contrast, the way relatives perceive us is somehow inevitably distorted by long-standing rivalries, inequalities and idealistic expectations. Although sometimes based on special intuition, the level of interpersonal awareness which exists between friends is, to a great extent, a product of intimacy and the process of mutual self-disclosure. If we understand our friends, it is at least in part because they have been prepared to reveal themselves to us.

Various expressions of commitment are fundamental ingredients of friendship. Proverbially, friends are expected to be loyal and faithful to the relationship. Indeed, accusations of fickleness or disloyalty are among the worst criticisms that can be levelled at friends, since both imply that the relationship is of no special or enduring value to them. Friends have many ways of

115

expressing commitment: for instance, by investing time, energy and resources in maintaining the relationship, by revealing distress at separation, via public or private declarations of commitment, or by defending the relationship from outside threats. There are also negative ways of expressing commitment – for example, by displaying jealousy when a friend embarks on a relationship with a third party – although possessiveness of this kind may spring from motives other than commitment. The important thing in friendship is that each participant demonstrates in some unequivocal way that the long-term survival of the relationship really matters (Duck 1983). It should also be emphasized that commitment in friendship is largely endogenous – that is, generated by the individuals themselves – whereas commitment towards relatives and, to a lesser extent, marital partners is strongly sanctioned by exogenous societal values and norms (Hinde 1979).

Mutual liking is another essential feature of friendship, although both 'liking' and 'love' are somewhat nebulous concepts which tend to be defined in terms of other factors, some of which have already been discussed. It is apparent, for example, that people are attracted to those who are similar to themselves, both in physical terms, background, attitudes and so on. Familiarity also tends to breed liking. Kindness and generosity are generally construed as likeable traits, although only if they are given freely without expectation of repayment. Similarly, if we like someone we will be more inclined to do things for them, without expecting the favour to be returned. We also tend to like those who trust and confide in us, and we are more likely to trust and confide in them as a result. Above all, liking needs to be reciprocated for close friendships to develop; it is important that our friends demonstrate that they like us at least as much as we like them. The growth of mutual liking therefore depends on a complex process of feedback and reinforcement, in which many different factors play a part (Hinde 1979). To the outside observer, it is generally obvious when two individuals like each other but the basis for their liking will generally depend on a complex array of mutually rewarding interpersonal interactions.

Finally, and perhaps most important of all, true friends are not allowed to harbour ulterior motives for being involved in the relationship. We expect our friends to like us for intrinsic aspects of our personalities, never for extrinsic factors, such as our physical appearance, our money, our power, or our business connections. The slightest hint of Machiavellianism in friendships – the smallest suggestion that we are being used for personal or material gain – instantly devalues the relationship and places it on an entirely different and more superficial footing. The ironical side of this component of friendship is that friends *do* use each other all the time, the only difference being that mutual exploitation within friendship is considered incidental to the relationship. We may take advantage of our friends (with their consent), but we are not supposed to embark on friendships with this objective in mind. Despite this apparently selfless element of friendship, however, many theories concerned with the function of such relationships assume that, because they are potentially costly to establish and maintain, people should balance their social involvements so as to maximize their own private interests (Huston and Burgess 1979). In other words, according to this view, we go to the trouble of forming and maintaining friendships because it is in our own selfish interests to do so. What, then, do people gain from their friendships, if not a promise of future assistance?

Recent research in the fields of psychosomatic medicine and psycho-immunology has provided abundant circumstantial evidence that humans suffer if deprived of opportunities to participate in close relationships with others. Symptoms of loneliness and social isolation include sleep disorders, anxiety, depression, headaches and increased susceptibility to a variety of both trivial and serious medical conditions (see Lynch 1977; Duck 1983; Serpell 1986). The precise mechanisms responsible for such affects are, as yet, poorly understood, although Duck (1983) has proposed various ways in which friendships and other close relationships may help to fulfil human social needs. According to Duck, friendships (i) provide the individual with a sense of belonging – a sense of being part of a social group or community; (ii) they act as a source of both physical and emotional support and assistance; (iii) they enhance our self-esteem by reassuring us of our own personal worth or value, and (iv) they increase our emotional and psychological stability by bolstering or propping up our attitudes, beliefs and opinions. Duck attaches greatest importance to the last function of friendship since, in his view, the human personality is an inherently fragile structure which needs constant reinforcement through interactions with like-minded others. By implication, then, the way the individual sees himself and hence his ability to cope with life is, to an important degree, a product of the way others perceive and treat him. Consequently, each of us strives to cultivate relationships with those whose behaviour engenders or reinforces positive self-perceptions, irrespective of whether or not those relationships are also useful in a practical or material sense. More to the point, perhaps, we cannot reliably obtain this kind of self-validation from those we suspect of ulterior motives.

To summarize, then, friendship is a label which tends to be applied to certain types of positive, intimate and relatively enduring relationship which are formed predominantly with individuals other than kin or sexual partners. Friendships are characterized by reciprocity – the exchange of gifts, favours, and positive affect – although friends are valued primarily for the emotional and psychological support they provide, rather than as sources of practical or material assistance. Friends tend to spend relatively large amounts of time in close proximity, and typically engage in a variety of different interactions with each other. These last two aspects of friendship, however, are highly variable and may be unreliable as indicators of friendship.

DO ANIMALS HAVE FRIENDS?

While studies of human sociality have traditionally fallen within the orbit of psychology, investigations of animal social relationships have been conducted primarily by biologists. In common with many social psychologists, however, ethologists, behavioural ecologists and sociobiologists also assume that social existence entails costs as well as benefits, and that the individual should therefore apportion its social involvements so as to maximize its own private gains (Kummer 1979). In the case of animals, however, the gains are generally expressed in terms of ultimate effects on individual survival and reproduction, rather than proximate benefits from social exchange (Alexander 1979). Evolutionary theory predicts that animals will only invest in those relationships which either directly or indirectly enhance their own 'fitness' – i.e. their own genetic representation in future generations – and, broadly speaking, this means that animals are constrained to act selfishly except in special circumstances. One such circumstance involves relationships with kin.

According to the theory of 'kin selection' (Hamilton 1964), individuals are selected not only to maximize their own survival and reproductive success but also that of their relatives, because relatives – to an extent proportional to their degree of relatedness – share genetic material in common. Natural selection will therefore favour individuals who help their kin, and it will be more likely to do so the closer the degree of relatedness between donor and recipient, and the smaller the cost thereby incurred by the donor. In practice, it seems that animals do tend to behave according to the predictions of the theory. Studies of non-human primates, for instance, consistently report that related individuals in social groups maintain greater proximity, groom each other at higher rates, and aid each other more in aggressive disputes than unrelated ones (Cheney and Seyfarth 1986). In other words, nepotism is the rule rather than the exception in animal societies.

Animals do, however, direct helping behaviour towards non-kin in certain situations. Unrelated male baboons, for example, have been observed forming temporary alliances in order to steal oestrus females from high-ranking males. While one attacks the male and so distracts him, the other mates with the female. According to Packer (1977), males who give aid in this way are more likely to receive assistance in return at some future date. Similarly, in experiments on free-living groups of vervet monkeys, Seyfarth and Cheney (1984) demonstrated that monkeys were more inclined to support a conspecific if they had been groomed by the same individual in the recent past. Both these examples may represent cases of so-called 'reciprocal altruism' (Trivers 1971); that is, the theory that an individual may benefit from helping another if there is a high probability that the act or some equivalent benefit will be reciprocated at some point in the future. The evolution of reciprocal altruism requires that individuals are able to recognize one another and remember their interactions, and that they tend to remain together in the same social group or locality for relatively long periods of time. Thus, superficially affectionate, altruistic acts, such as grooming in non-human primates, may conceal essentially Machiavellian intentions. In many species, high-ranking females are groomed much more often than low-ranking ones, and sometimes subordinates

119

compete for the opportunity to groom their superiors. This behaviour is widely interpreted as attempts by low-ranking animals to win the approval and support of potentially powerful allies (Walters and Seyfarth, 1987).

There are, of course, a variety of other circumstances in which the benefits of co-operative or mutualistic interactions with non-kin are more immediate. In some species of tropical firefly, for example, males aggregate and synchronize their visual displays in order to attract females (Otte 1980). Similarly, in many species of social carnivore, such as lions or hunting dogs, non-relatives co-operate when hunting large prey (Bertram 1978). In both cases, the net benefit to the individual from co-operating is thought to be greater than that which could be obtained by acting alone. The term 'co-operation' is used here in the broad descriptive sense to mean individuals acting together to achieve shared goals.

Although such examples indicate that many animals are capable of establishing positive, mutually-rewarding relationships with individuals who are neither related nor sexual partners, they do not qualify as friendships, either because they are not associated with enduring affiliative bonds, or because they only exist to serve the private ambitions of those involved. A few examples of 'friendly' relationships among animals, however, are less easily dismissed in these terms.

Juvenile vervet monkeys, for instance, sometimes form special relationships with unrelated peers which involve frequent mutual grooming and playful interactions. Lee (1981) refers to such relationships as friendships, although their context is relatively specific. In so far as these relationships resemble so-called 'friendships' among young children (see Rubin 1980), the label is perhaps justified, although the early ethological term 'Kumpan' or 'social companion' might be more appropriate under the circumstances (see Lorenz 1935). Outside of the breeding season, female squirrel monkeys also form special, semi-exclusive relationships with one or two other females. Vaitl (1978) refers to these as F-class relationships instead of friendships, and it is unclear whether the 'F' signifies females or friends. F-class relationships are characterized by frequent proximity and physical contact in the form of 'huddling', and by the active exclusion of other individuals. Unfortunately, Vaitl's observations were conducted using captive groups, and she does not indicate whether preferred partners, either in the wild or in captivity, are related or unrelated.

Goodall (1986) uses the term 'friendships' to describe enduring positive relationships among chimpanzees 'characterized by two-way affiliative, supportive interactions.' The majority of such relationships, however, occur either between mothers and their adult daughters or between adult brothers. Male chimpanzees occasionally form long-term, co-operative social bonds with other unrelated males, but such relationships differ from typical human friendships in so far as the animals involved usually occupy very different social ranks. Chimpanzee males use their allies primarily as sources of support and reassurance during disputes with other males, although 'friends' will actively seek each other's company in non-threatening situations, and may scream or whimper in distress when they lose contact with a chosen companion. Although female chimpanzees almost never form friendly relationships with unrelated females in the wild, they will apparently do so in captive groups. Goodall suggests that, because captive females cannot absent themselves from social conflicts within such groups as they would in the wild, they may be under pressure to establish more complex networks of social affiliation as a means, so to speak, of keeping the peace.

Smuts (1985) has also elected to use the word 'friendship' to describe a particular type of positive, long-term relationship which often develops between male and female olive baboons. Sub-adult male baboons generally transfer out of their natal groups to join others, while females tend to remain where they are. As a result of this pattern of dispersal, the males and females within a troop tend to be unrelated. Despite this, females establish enduring, affiliative relationships with particular males which persist, sometimes for many years, even when the female is not reproductively active. These special relationships share many features in common with human friendships. They are characterized by proximity – females spend relatively large amounts of time close to their chosen partners – and by physical intimacy in the form of grooming. In a troop containing 18 adult males, for example, each non-oestrus female performed most of her grooming with only one, two or, rarely, three or more different males. Baboons also tend to form their friendships with individuals of similar rank to themselves,

121

although males and females differ in the number of friends they possess. Females usually have only one or two friends, while males vary from having as many as eight female friends, to having none at all. Older males who have been in the troop for a long time tend to have more friends than newcomers, but high-ranking individuals are no more likely to have friends than subordinates. Females generally play a more active role in maintaining these relationships – seeking proximity with male friends rather than vice versa, and grooming more than they are groomed – but males also display a degree of possessiveness. Males, for instance, have been observed showing signs of apparent jealousy when their friends engage in friendly interactions with rival males.

Baboon friendships appear to confer a variety of benefits on both participants. Males defend their female friends from attacks by other troop members, and may even 'punish' other individuals for attacking a friend when the incident was witnessed but the male was not in a position to offer immediate protection. Males are also highly solicitous towards their friend's youngest infants; intervening if other males approach or if the mother or infant become distressed at the attentions of other females and juveniles. As the infant matures, male friends will also undertake some of the care-taking duties of the mother; comforting the infant when it is distressed, allowing it access to choice food items, and so on. Surprisingly, however, in only about half of the friendships observed was the male likely to have been the father of his friend's infant and, where the relationships involved a female infant, males displayed no sexual interest in their adopted 'daughters' when the latter reached puberty. In return for their assistance, it seems that males, on average, have a higher probability of siring their friend's next infant; female baboons, it was found, consistently preferred mating with male friends when they next came into oestrus, and would actively avoid mating with other males. It is also probable that new males transferring into a troop are accepted and assimilated more rapidly if they are good at cultivating friendships with resident females.

Smuts (1985) justifiably regards these special relationships between male and female baboons as the product of female choice. In other words, by grooming and preferentially mating with certain males, females ensure protection and support for themselves and their infants. If this is the case, however, females are presumably assessing males for their potential as helpers, and their friendship is conditional on the outcome of this assessment process. In which case, the relationship appears more calculated than we believe human friendships to be. Males, conversely, participate in friendships primarily in return for reproductive benefits, and this too is uncharacteristic of friendships among humans. In short, baboon friendships seem more closely analogous to human marital alliances than true friendships.

From the point of view of comparison, however, it is important to re-emphasize that human friendships are nowhere near as selfless and altruistic as we may like to believe. As already stated, people appear to derive considerable practical, social and emotional benefits from their friendships, and most of these relationships would founder in the absence of reciprocity. In other words, the apparently unique human habit of forming friendships with unrelated individuals may also, like its nearest animal equivalents, involve a high degree of mutualistic self-interest.

As to why humans have evolved friendships and other animals have not, one can only speculate. Alexander (1979) has argued that, in traditional tribal societies, most close, reciprocal relationships are formed between genetic relatives, and that non-relatives are only included in this social network in more complex societies where the tribal or clan system has broken down. Indeed, he argues that friendships are essentially artifacts of urban existence where people are forced into close contact with non-relatives who then assume roles that cause them to be treated as if they were genetic relatives. This would appear to be a serious over-simplification, however, since relationships with friends are qualitatively different from those with relatives. Goodall's (1986) observations on captive female chimpanzees are perhaps more instructive. The highly interdependent nature of human society may, like the bars of a cage, constitute a form of captivity in which natural selection has favoured individuals who are able to extend their network of affiliative relationships beyond the normal boundaries of kinship and sexual alliances. Since humans are long-lived, and it is impossible for the individual to predict whose support is likely to be most useful over an entire lifetime, the simplest and safest strategy may be to form these friendly relationships with peers whose attitudes, opinions and personalities are most compatible with one's own. Careful mutual assessment would necessarily form an essential part of the negotiation, enabling individuals to decide whether prospective friends were committed to the long-term survival and success of the relationship, or merely in it to satisfy short-term private ambitions. This idea would help to explain the apparent need to disguise obvious or immediate self-interest in friendships.

MAN'S BEST FRIEND?

Although animals do not appear to form true friendships under natural conditions, it is clear that they can form durable, non-sexual bonds with unrelated individuals in captivity or under domestication. Such attachments may also transcend species boundaries. It is well known, for example, that horses isolated from conspecifics in stables will form powerful, non-sexual attachments with substitute animals such as goats or sheep, and many pet-owners observe affectionate bonds developing between cats and dogs in the same household. Anecdotal accounts of similar cross-species relationships, involving everything from cats and rats to cats and gorillas, are also widely reported in the literature (see Serpell 1986). The existence of such relationships provides ample evidence that many animals, like humans, possess social needs which are independent of long- or short-term material rewards. Whether or not such relationships should be referred to as friendships, however, is entirely debatable. The problem is that animals cannot tell us about their relationships, so we have no way of assessing whether the things they gain from such alliances are necessarily equivalent or even similar to what humans derive from friendship. The apparent importance of human friendships as sources of personality support and self-esteem would, however, imply a fundamental difference between the two types of relationship.

Captive and domestic animals also establish close social bonds with humans, although their behaviour towards people within such relationships is often very different from that which we normally associate with friends. Most companion animals or pets, for instance, are socialized to their human owners during early development and the unequal and highly-dependent relationship which results is maintained throughout the animal's life. As a consequence, these animals tend to behave in either an infantile or a highly subordinate way towards their human partners. Adult cats, for example, consistently respond to their human owners in a manner very similar to that shown by kittens towards their mothers, while adult dogs behave in essentially the same way as their wild ancestors would towards dominant pack members (Serpell 1986). In neither case would 'friendship' constitute an appropriate description of the relationship, at least from the animal's viewpoint.

Despite the apparent contradiction, however, such relationships may indeed qualify as friendships from the perspective of the human participant. While the relationship with a pet animal is non-egalitarian and obviously limited at the level of communication, the behaviour of pets towards their owners may both mimic and exaggerate many of the most important aspects of friendship. Companion animals, such as dogs and cats, for example, actively seek physical proximity and contact with their owners, and engage in a variety of mutually pleasurable interactions – play, grooming or petting, walking, sleeping together, and so on. Apart from working dogs or horses, pets offer little in the way of practical support, although many dog-owners claim to feel safer and more secure in the animal's company. In terms of emotional support, however, they may be more valuable. Most owners report that their animals are very sensitive to their moods, and that they increase their level of affection and attention when the owner is feeling unwell or unhappy. Pets, in other words, are good at adjusting the frequency, patterning and quality of their interactions to suit the owner's expectations. Relationships with pets are also generally extremely positive and affectionate, and usually free of conflicts or competition. Indeed, the fact that pets cannot speak means that they are incapable of judging or criticizing their owners' attitudes or behaviour (Serpell 1986).

As far as reciprocity is concerned, companion animals are closer to children than friends. Owners expect love and affection from their pets, in return for food and care, rather than repayment in kind. The relationship is therefore complementary rather than reciprocal, in the same sense that relationships between parents and offspring are complementary (Hinde 1979). The relationship, however, is exceptionally intimate, at least at the physical level, and many owners reportedly use their pets as confidants. Again the sensitivity of pets to their owner's behaviour is probably important;

animals may not understand what is said to them, but they often behave as if they do. Rightly or wrongly, the owner may therefore come to the conclusion that the animal 'understands' him better than most people do, and he can also be confident that his secret disclosures to the pet will never be betrayed or revealed (Serpell 1986).

Various expressions of commitment and love are among the most endearing aspects of companion animals. The loyalty and fidelity of the dog towards its master is, after all, legendary, and few things are less gratifying to many dog-owners than an animal which fails to differentiate socially between themselves and other people. In a spurious attempt to link canine personality with phylogenetic origins, Konrad Lorenz (1954), for example, distinguished between animals of wolf and jackal ancestry. The former is portrayed as a canine paragon; mature in outlook, and utterly faithful to one master, while the latter is denigrated as infantile, and indiscriminately friendly and obsequious towards everyone it meets. Lorenz later admitted to getting his facts wrong – all dogs are probably descended from wolves – but his sentiments are doubtless still shared by a majority of people. Most dogs and many cats also show some degree of distress when involuntarily separated from their owners, and, according to a recent American study, many also display symptoms of jealousy when the owner gives too much attention to a third party (Mathes and Deuger 1982).

Finally, pets excel in the apparent selflessness and sincerity of their affection. As Aldous Huxley once wrote, 'to his dog, every man is Napoleon' regardless of his race, creed, colour, beliefs, attitudes, status, affluence, or physical handicaps. The dog's liking for its owner is therefore unconditional, and unsullied by any suspicion of ulterior motives. Indeed, studies have shown that dogs form their attachments for people independent of physical rewards or punishments (Scott 1963). This trustworthy element of canine friendship may be especially valuable to those, such as the wealthy and powerful, whose fear of being exploited is justifiably greatest. As one nineteenth-century novelist put it, 'those who are great or eminent in any way find the world full of parasites, toadies, liars, fawners, hypocrites: the incorruptible candour, loyalty and honour of the dog are to such like water in a barren place to a thirsty traveller' (Ouida 1891). Cats, interestingly, have a not

126

entirely deserved reputation for being Machiavellian in their affections, which may explain why many dog-lovers are suspicious of cats, and why many cat-lovers suspect dog-lovers of having ego problems.

Either way, it is apparent that the company of animals fulfils many of the requirements of true friendship, and that the current popularity of pets is a reflection of this phenomenon. Companion animals may do little to reinforce their owner's personalities and opinions, and may contribute nothing in terms of practical support or a sense of belonging. But, when it comes to enhancing self-esteem and a sense of personal worth, such relationships appear to compete on equal terms with the closest and most rewarding of human friendships. As Horace Walpole, the Fourth Earl of Orford, observed:

> Sense and fidelity are wonderful recommendations; and when one meets with them, and can be confident that one is not imposed upon, I cannot think that two additional legs are any drawback. At least I know that I have had friends who would never have vexed or betrayed me, if they had walked on all fours.

CONCLUSIONS

Human friendships share many features in common with certain social relationships in other species, particularly among non-human primates. The requirement, however, that friends should value the relationship itself above and beyond the gratification of personal ambitions, seems to be unique, and is uncharacteristic of analogous relationships among animals living under natural conditions. Human friendships, and the particular rules of conduct associated with them, probably evolved in the face of increasing social pressures which necessitated the formation of durable, reciprocal alliances with individuals other than kin or sexual partners. Since such alliances are expected to last a long time, perhaps for the lifetime of the individual, the process of friendship-formation places the emphasis on mutual liking, trust and compatibility, rather than on the prospect of immediate or even deferred material gains.

Despite the apparent absence of true friendships among animals, humans are able to derive many of the social and emotional benefits of friendship from relationships with animals, especially dogs, cats and other household pets. Perhaps because they involve other species, and therefore appear superficially counterfeit, such relationships between humans and animals have been largely ignored by ethologists and social psychologists. This is, perhaps, regrettable, since their particular differences and similarities may reveal a great deal about both the meaning and the limits of friendship.

REFERENCES

Alexander, R. D. (1979) 'Natural selection and social exchange', in Burgess, R. L. and Huston, T. L. (eds) *Social Exchange in Developing Relationships*, New York and London: Academic Press, pp. 197–221.

Altman, I. and Taylor, D. A. (1973) *Social Penetration: the Development of Interpersonal Relationships*, New York: Holt, Rinehart & Winston.

Bertram, B. (1978) 'Living in groups', in Krebs, J. R. and Davies, N. B. (eds) *Behavioural Ecology: An Evolutionary Approach*, Oxford: Blackwell Scientific, pp. 64–96.

Cheney, D. L. and Seyfarth, R. M. (1986) 'The recognition of social alliances by vervet monkeys', *Animal Behaviour* 34: 1722–31.

Duck, S. (1983) *Friends for Life*, Brighton: Harvester Press.

Essock-Vitale, S. M. and McGuire, M. T. (1985) 'Women's lives viewed from an evolutionary perspective. 2. Patterns of helping', *Ethology and Sociobiology* 6: 155–73.

Goodall, J. (1986) *The Chimpanzees of Gombe*, Cambridge, Mass.: Belknap Press.

Hamilton, W. D. (1964) 'The genetical evolution of social behaviour', *Journal of Theoretical Biology*, 7: 1–32.

Hinde, R. A. (1979) *Towards Understanding Relationships*, New York and London: Academic Press.

Huston, T. L. and Burgess, R. L. (1979) 'Social exchange in developing relationships: an overview', in Burgess, R. L. and Huston, T. L. (eds) *Social Exchange in Developing Relationships*, New York and London: Academic Press, pp. 3–28.

Kimmel, D. C. (1979) 'Relationship initiation and development: a life-span developmental approach', in Burgess, R. L. and Huston, T. L. (eds) *Social Exchange in Developing Relationships*, New York and London: Academic Press, pp. 351–77.

Kummer, H. (1979) 'On the value of social relationships to non-human primates: a heuristic scheme', in von Cranach, M., Foppa, K., Lepenies, W. and Ploog, D. (eds) *Human Ethology: Claims and Limits of a New Discipline*, Cambridge: Cambridge University Press.

Lee, P. C. (1981) *Ecological and Social Influences on the Development of Vervet Monkeys* (Cercopithecus aethiops), Ph. D. Diss., Cambridge: University of Cambridge.

Lorenz, K. (1935)'Der Kumpan in der Umwelt des Vogels', *Journal für Ornithologie* 80.

——(1954) *Man Meets Dog*, London: Methuen.

Lynch, J. J. (1977) *The Broken Heart: the Medical Consequences of Loneliness*, New York: Basic Books.

Mathes, E. W. and Deuger, D. I. (1982) 'Jealousy, a creation of human culture?' *Psychological Reports* 51: 251–4.

Mugford, R. A. (1980) 'The social significance of pet-ownership', in Corson, S. A. and O'Leary Corson, E. (eds) *Ethology and Nonverbal Communication in Mental Health*, Oxford: Pergamon Press, pp. 111–22.

Otte, D. (1980) 'On theories of flash synchronization in fireflies', *American Naturalist* 116: 587–90.

Ouida (1891) 'Dogs and their affections', *North American Review* 153: 317.

Packer, C. (1977) 'Reciprocal altruism in *Papio anubis*', *Nature* 265: 441–3.

Ritvo, H. (1987) *The Animal Estate*, Cambridge, Mass.: Harvard University Press.

Rubin, Z. (1980) *Children's Friendships* London: Fontana.

Scott, J. P. (1963) 'The process of primary socialization in canine and human infants', *Monographs of the Society for Research on Child Development* 28: 1–47.

Serpell, J. A. (1986) *In the Company of Animals*, Oxford: Basil Blackwell.

Seyfarth, R. M. and Cheney, D. L. (1984) 'Grooming, alliances, and reciprocal altruism in vervet monkeys', *Nature* 308: 541–3.

Singer, P. (1983) *Animal Liberation*, Wellingborough, Northants: Thorsons.

Smuts, B. B. (1985) *Sex and Friendship in Baboons*, New York: Aldine.

Trivers, R. L. (1971) 'The evolution of reciprocal altruism', *Quarterly Review of Biology* 46: 35–57.

Vaitl, E. (1978) 'Nature and implications of the complexly organized social system in primates', in Chivers, D. J. and Herbert, J. (eds) *Recent Advances in Primatology*, New York and London: Academic Press, pp. 17–30.

Walters, J. R. and Seyfarth, R. M. (1987) 'Conflict and co-operation', in Smuts, B. B., Cheney, D. L., Seyfarth, R. M., Wrangham, R. W., and Struhsaker, T. T. (eds) *Primate Societies*, Chicago: Chicago University Press, pp. 306–17.

Chapter Eight

FRIENDSHIP AND THE SOCIAL ORDER

STEPHANIE GARRETT

Relationships with friends have the following distinctive features: they are voluntary *(by contrast with relationships with neighbours except when these are also friends); they are* intimate *in the way that relationships with acquaintances are not; they are not based on ties of kinship or legal responsibility; and they are not necessarily* enduring.
(Willmott 1987)

If we want to know how far the social order is sustained by friendship, it seems crucial to establish the answers to a number of questions. Firstly, to what extent do friendships confine themselves to class and other like-status social groups: if there is evidence that they do not, it might perhaps be thought that the social order, as based on class, gender and age, is subverted rather than supported by friendship. Secondly, is there any evidence of differences in friendship styles within social groups – men and women, middle and working class, for example? What evidence, if any, exists about the value placed on friendship by different groups of people? Thirdly, do friendships survive when the personal circumstances of individuals alter – either over time, or dramatically, as the result of factors such as divorce, job promotion or marriage: societies constantly change, and some would maintain that the pace of social change is constantly accelerating in western societies.

The answers to these questions which form the basis of this chapter relate entirely to western societies. This is because studies of non-western cultures focus almost entirely on kinship and make no mention of friendship at all. Friendship *per se* is not a subject which has been researched by many sociologists, even in western societies, so it is actually very difficult to provide satisfactory answers to the questions in any case. The emphasis in friendship research from psychologists has been very much on subjects such as success and failure in personal relationships, practical advice on how friendship skills may be developed in order that satisfying relationships may be built. In sociology, research on friendship in western societies has remained a secondary topic: the emphasis in most studies has been on kinship rather than friendship ties. This could be, as Willmott (1987) maintains, because friendship research is extremely difficult to do; there is no agreed definition about what a 'friend' actually is, or about what 'friendship' means – and this helps account for the fact that it is no easy task to try to measure the significance or relevance of friendship. 'Friends' really do signify very different things to different people. The researcher who wishes to study friendship patterns is therefore confronted with a major problem: how to conceptualize, operationalize and measure 'friendship'. The difficulties involved in this are so great that, as Willmott comments, the few researchers who have tackled the subject have tried to avoid the issue by focusing only on limited categories of potential friends, or employing taken-for-granted categories such as 'close friends' (which again have multiple meanings) – as a result, it is difficult to compare studies. Willmott's recent study *Friendship Networks and Social Support* (1987) is one of the few which focuses specifically on friendship. Using data gathered from interviews with 163 married people of working- and middle-class origins with dependent children living in the same London suburb, it attempts to describe their friendship patterns in detail and to identify the various ways in which friends provide one another with help and support. It identifies friends as those individuals the respondents had met socially in a six-month period; in terms of the help (of a practical kind) given to respondents in a similar period; and in terms of the respondents' own definitions. A central aim of Willmott's research was to devise and test methods of studying friendship and he recognizes that his operationalization has limitations.

Given the state of friendship research it is clearly difficult to provide other than tentative answers to the questions posed at the start of the chapter. This is an area in which more investigation is badly needed. However, on the basis of the work that has so far been done (however limited) I would argue the following: that in western industrial societies in general, friendships patterns do support the wider social order of class, gender and generation: that members of these groups have different patterns of sociability and friendship. With some rare exceptions, when a person's circumstances alter, so do that person's friendships. For some social groups – notably women and teenagers of both sexes – there is some evidence from sociological studies that friendship plays a central part in answering needs not met by other social institutions such as the family or workplace.

CLASS

There is no substantial evidence from any studies of the existence or significance of friendships which cross class lines in western industrial societies (class as measured by occupation). Middle-class people tend to make friends with other middle-class people, and working-class people with other working-class people. There appear to be a number of necessary conditions for the formation of friendships (Duck 1980; Willmott 1987) which may explain why this is so. These are: opportunity, having something in common, mutual attraction, and having the necessary social skills. It is likely that, because of residence and work patterns, middle- and working-class people will have more opportunities to come into contact with those from the same general category as themselves; it is also more likely that people from the same class background will make friends with one another, rather than with individuals who have a very different material standard of living and differing values. As Stacey *et al.* (1975) pointed out in their study of Banbury, generally persons of widely different social levels do not interact with one another except in chance encounters or in certain well-defined relationships (e.g. shopkeeper/client, doctor/patient). Heath (1981) points out that, according to data from the Oxford Social Mobility Group study, the tendency for people to select friends from their own class is highest in Class 1 (professionals) and Classes 6 and 7 (semi and unskilled manual workers).

The Oxford data also shows, however, that a proportion of those in Britain who are socially mobile do have friends from a wide range of social backgrounds. Although most of the upwardly mobile draw their friends from their current social class, a substantial number retain working-class friends as well (the major finding of the study was that there had been an increase in upward social mobility as a result of significant changes in the occupational structure, particularly the expansion of the 'service class'). The Oxford study supports the view that there is no distinct cleavage between classes regarding friendship – rather the boundaries are blurred and fuzzy. This view, however, applies only to some upwardly mobile individuals, and not to the majority of the population.

Most sociological studies of friendship have suggested that not only do working- and middle-class friendships not cross class lines, but also that within each class the styles of friendship are very different. Allan's (1979) review of British research in this area describes the studies as indicating that friendship is actually more significant to middle- rather than working-class people – for the latter, relatives and kin are all-important. Working-class people have fewer friends than middle-class people, and the friendships are of a more limited character, stressing specific activities rather than intimacy, and with contact taking place mainly outside rather than inside the home. The friendships of working-class people are also, according to Allan's review, much more likely than those of middle-class people to be segregated along gender lines (confirmed also by Tunstall (1962), Dennis (1956)).

Willmott's (1987) research into the friendship networks and social support of a sample of people in London suggests that, although class does continue to influence friendship, the differences noted by earlier researchers are not as marked as they used to be. Middle-class couples in this study were found to have larger networks of friends than working-class couples – however, the friends that the working-class couples did meet were seen as frequently as middle-class people saw their friends: working-class people thus made up for smaller networks of friends by seeing them more frequently. A large majority of the friends of both working- and middle-class couples lived relatively near to them and there were no differences in the frequency of meetings. However, middle-class couples had more non-local friends and saw them more often (they were more likely to have cars, which made such visiting easier). There was evidence of friendships in both classes being segregated along gender lines but this was much more common among the working-class couples. Again, although couples in all classes reported having friends in for a meal and going out with friends for a drink, the proportion of middle-class people citing the former as a popular activity was much higher than for the working-class couples, and the proportion of working-class couples citing the latter as a popular activity with friends was much higher than among the middle-class couples.

Willmott's study also looked at the help received from friends, relatives and neighbours by the sample families: it found that middle-class people relied on friends more than working-class people for help with a child's illness and babysitting, while people from both classes looked to friends for help with house maintenance. For both classes, friends were more important than relatives or neighbours in providing help with shopping, house maintenance, 'keeping an eye on the home' and talking over personal problems. For many individuals in the middle and working class, local friends – and especially those who started as 'just neighbours' – played a crucial role in providing practical support on a day-to-day basis, with friends in general being important as 'confidants'.

Both working- and middle-class people in this study recognized the difference between 'close friends' and other friends. Respondents were asked by Willmott to pick out the one aspect of friendship that they valued most: 29 per cent replied 'someone you can always turn to for help'; 21 per cent said it was 'someone you can trust'; 21 per cent maintained it was 'someone you can talk to freely about anything'; 18 per cent said it was 'someone whose company you can enjoy'. Thirty per cent of middle-class respondents, as opposed to six per cent of working-class respondents, rated enjoyment of a friend's company as very important.

How can the differences in friendship styles be explained? Willmott (1987) argues that material resources are a crucial factor. The greater affluence of middle-class couples makes it possible for them to entertain at home frequently, and actually to have a home in which such entertaining can more comfortably take place. It also enables them to have cars (often more than one per family) which makes them more mobile and able to visit friends at a distance more conveniently, as well as creating greater opportunities for wider social mixing. A second factor is level of education. This was also found to be relevant to friendship patterns by Fischer (1982) in an American study. It seems both in Britain and the USA (and probably by implication similar societies) that more highly educated people have larger numbers of friends. This may be because education widens opportunities and increases a person's chances of geographical mobility, especially in an academic career. A third factor is class traditions relating to friendship. Young and Willmott (1962) found in a British study that historical socio-economic conditions led to a friendship style among working-class people centred on activity outside the home and on male-female segregation. These traditions survive, according to recent studies. Goldthorpe and Lockwood (1969) found that some of their affluent Luton manual workers, in another British study, 'remained restricted to working class styles of sociability. . .in the formation of friendships they are guided neither by middle class norms nor aided by middle class social skills.' For these people 'making friends' was not at all a typical feature of their way of life – moreover, there were few cross-class friendships, even in mixed class housing areas. Gavron's (1966) study of middle- and working-class London housewives noted that friendship styles differed by class and that friendships were still much more likely to be segregated by gender among the working rather than the middle class.

Traditionally, working-class people have lived in close-knit communities in which, for the most part, friendships were ready-made and took second place to kin relations: in such communities there were thus no well-developed traditions relating to friendship-making skills. Working-class culture, therefore, has not equipped people with these skills, and this could be why in new communities (and there is ample evidence that the old close-knit communities are disappearing) working-class people make fewer friends, and according to some (Gavron 1966), experience loneliness. Lack of friendship-making skills is also associated with loneliness by Fischer (1981) – this lack, rather than whether or not an individual lived in a rural or an urban area, was found by him to be associated with loneliness. Willmott (1987) found that couples who lacked support (from relatives and friends) were mainly working-class people without experience of further education and often without cars, but comments that there is no obvious explanation why these couples had not acquired friendship-making skills when other similar working-class couples had done so.

Willmott maintains that 'styles of friendship which were once characteristic of middle-class people are becoming more common among working-class people'. This, he argues, is shown by the decrease in dependence of working-class people on kin, the increasing likelihood of working-class people entertaining their friends at home, and some evidence suggesting that the degree of male-female segregation in friendship among the working class is less than in the past. He maintains that a 'principle of stratified diffusion' is operating with respect to friendship: friendship styles once the exclusive preserve of the higher classes are percolating downwards through the class system. This has been made possible by better standards of living, higher incomes, changes in working hours and changes in the social lives of men and women. As a result, traditional working-class values and norms have weakened. Willmott's view here would be seriously challenged by Marxist and feminist sociologists, who argue that class and gender differences remain fundamental in western industrial capitalist societies.

The available evidence, then, suggests that friendship largely sustains the social order, at least as far as the class structure is concerned. However, the evidence is limited and has nothing at all to say about friendship patterns among the élite upper classes of Britain or any other western society. One area for investigation here might be the extent to which the 'old boy' or 'old school tie' network in this group functions as a friendship network as well as a job placement network. This would be a fascinating area for research, were researchers able to gain access to the group concerned – problems of access to powerful and privileged groups being well established for investigators.

GENDER

The previous section has already commented on the way in which friendships among men and women are more clearly segregated by gender among the working rather than the middle classes. However, there is some evidence which suggests that there are differences in male and female friendships styles which cut across class lines. I would argue that the available evidence on male and female friendships is that they sustain existing gender relationships in western societies, and in so doing support this aspect of the social order.

Firstly, there is almost no evidence of cross-gender friendship. Men make friends with other men, and women make friends with other women. The slight exception to this is the tendency of some couples to meet other couples as friends, noted by Willmott (1987) among couples with dependent children – nevertheless, when these couples as individuals met friends, the friend was invariably of the same sex. Bott (1957) related the tendency of friends to meet as couples to the degree of inequality in the marriage, and argued that there was a general trend for couples with less segregated conjugal roles (mainly middle-class couples in this study) to meet their friends as couples, whereas those with highly segregated conjugal roles would be much more likely to meet same-sex friends separately.

Willmott's (1987) study noted, however, that men and women had roughly the same number of friends, although women's friends were less likely to know one another than men's friends were. Women tended to see their friends more on a one-to-one basis than men, and were more likely to meet them in the home than men. 'The commonest meeting places for male friends were pubs, often after work, or sports and social clubs. When women met outside the home this seemed mainly to be outside the children's school, at the shops or at a local group such as a keep-fit class or mother and toddler group'. Most of the women in Willmott's sample were in the 'traditional' gender role of full-time housewife/mother while the men were all involved in paid work outside the home. The higher number of meetings the women had with their friends is explained largely in terms of the greater opportunities for meeting that their situation gave rise to.

Gavron (1966) found that seeing friends was largely a day-time as opposed to an evening activity for working-class women, and that middle-class women were much less likely than working-class women to be satisfied by friendship based on domestic matters alone. Middle-class women's friendships centred more around clubs and organizations (such as the Women's Institute and National Housewives' Register) than did working-class women's friendships. Many studies have indicated that women's greater activity in kinship networks is paralleled by their greater activity in friendship networks. Willmott (1987) found that women not only telephoned and wrote to their friends more often than men did to theirs, but that they played a central role in arranging occasions when couples met as friends. If a couple's friendship with another couple ended, it was usually because of the woman's wishes, which were accepted by their male partners. The role of women in keeping friendships going in this way was often consciously recognized by Willmott's working- and middle-class respondents – a role described by the author as 'the social secretary's role'. Women's greater knowledge of kinship networks is perhaps paralleled by their greater knowledge of friendship networks. The socialization of women in terms of traditional femininity as defined in western societies prepares them to accept this role, and leads to women placing much importance on the value of friendship and relationships.

Willmott's study also suggests that there is a difference in the type of practical help given by men and women to their same-sex friends. The most important form of help given among women friends in his study was looking after children during the day, and especially important in giving this sort of help were local female neighbours who had become friends. Gavron (1966) and Oakley (1975) have both recognized the significance of this kind of support to housewives/mothers. In addition to the practical nature of the help, the emotional support involved is often crucial in stemming or counteracting the feelings of depression and isolation so frequently experienced by women in this situation. The suggestion is that such women receive little in the way of support from their partners, relatives or other institutions. Recent research by feminists does indeed suggest that there is little 'equality' in marriage in western societies with regard to childcare and housework, and that it remains an expectation on the part of most men and many women in these societies that these areas of family life are 'women's work'. In the absence of other support, that provided by women for their women friends is crucial. Ironically, perhaps, women who do rely a great deal on support from their women friends in this situation may be less likely to demand support from their male partners, and it could thus be the case that women's friendships reinforce the notion that housework/childcare are 'women's business'. The unequal division of labour between the sexes in the family is thus sustained.

And yet women's friendships are frequently dismissed by men as trivial and centring on gossip.

There is some evidence that some female friendships endure despite changes in the situation of individual women. However, this is also true of male friendship. Some friendships do survive throughout life, even when the friends do not meet regularly, or when they are separated by great geographical distances. The survival of such friendships is not well documented, however, and would seem to be the exception rather than the rule. It also appears to be the case that both men and women make distinctions between 'close' and other friends, although this is better documented with regard to men. Morse and Marks (1985) found that Australian males routinely distinguished between 'mates' and 'friends' – a 'mate' being a non-intimate friend. Allan (1979) in a study of an East Anglian village found that men saw 'mates' as friends to do things with – time spent with them was activity- rather than talk-centred. Ward (1966) argues that 'mateship' as opposed to 'friendship' is essentially a casual relationship – 'a form of exclusive egalitarian male bonding that develops in response to living without women'. Allan, however, found that men have mates whether or not they also have female company. Morse and Marks back up the idea that 'mateship' is more casual with their finding that work problems would often be discussed with mates (but not personal problems) and that friends, but never mates, might be asked for a financial loan or advice.

Gender socialization in western societies emphasizes the idea that the sexes have very different interests and concerns, and also encourages each sex to see the other in primarily sexual terms. The way in which the mass media in these societies objectify women has been particularly well documented. Members of the opposite sex are encouraged by western values to see one another primarily as potential sexual partners rather than as friends – indeed, socialization could be said to stress the view that sexual relationships and friendship do not 'go' together. By the age of five, children's friendship patterns already show a preference on the part of both boys and girls for same-sex friends: in numerous observational studies of children playing in nursery schools this has also been demonstrated (Belotti 1975; Adelman 1980). The preference for same-sex friends is heightened in adolescence.

On the basis of the evidence available, it would seem that the existing balance of power and inequality between males and females in western societies is strongly sustained by the friendship patterns of men and women.

AGE

If, as research has suggested, the stage of life which a person has reached is a major influence on their informal relationships, we should not be very surprised to discover that friendships do not, in general, cross age boundaries in western societies, given the relationship between chronological age and stage of life. People tend to select as friends those at the same stage and those of the same age as themselves. Duck (1980) has pointed out that one of the main purposes of friendship is to give support and validity to a person's personality and thoughts. Teenagers, for example, mainly choose other teenagers as friends, as a study of 11–15 year-olds in the English town of Lancaster (quoted in Duck) shows. Schofield (1965) argues that an important function of teenage friendship is to provide teenagers with information about sex – information which, for many British male and female teenagers at least, is often not provided either by the family in the shape of parents, or by the education system. In this respect teenage friendship answers needs of teenagers which are not met by the major social institutions with which they are involved. Most teenagers, like most adults, make friends with people of the same sex as themselves. McRobbie (1985) suggests that a central aspect of the friendships between teenage girls is the discussion of boys, sex and romance; yet as Griffin (1985) shows in her study of 15–16 year-old girls in Birmingham, when a teenage girl acquires a 'steady' boyfriend (this being a central aim for most teenage girls), contact with her 'best' girl friend often decreases dramatically – frequently to the chagrin of the 'best' friend (the process is termed 'deffing out' by the girls). However, as Willis (1977) shows, 'deffing out' is not something that happens to boys – they continue to see and spend time with their male friends, with or without the 'steady' girlfriend. Patterns of friendship here are thus related to gender as well as to age, with female friendships reflecting the dependency of females on males.

Willmott's (1987) study showed a slightly higher tendency for middle-, as opposed to working-class, people to have friends of a similar age to themselves. In general, people's 'best' friends were born in the same decade as themselves – three-quarters of all 'best' friends fell into this category. Age peers, argues Willmott, are 'close' enough to be able to act as effective confidants in ways that may be difficult for those of a very different age group, or for relatives – the latter, having detailed and long-standing memories, may be unable to see the individual as anything other than a daughter, brother, or parent, for example. Similar-age friends are extremely important in providing emotional and personal support and in facilitating an individual's development. This immediately suggests why friendships and peer group relationships are so important to teenagers who are experiencing the transition from childhood to adulthood, which involves becoming increasingly independent of one's family of origin.

REFERENCES

Adelman, C. (1980) in Delamont, S. (ed.) *The Sociology of Women*, London: Allen & Unwin.

Allan, G. A. (1979) *A Sociology of Friendship and Kinship*, London: Allen & Unwin.

Belotti, E. (1975) *Little Girls*, London: Writers' and Readers' Publishing Co-operative.

Bott, E. (1957) *The Family and Social Network*, London: Tavistock.

Dennis, N. (1956) *Coal is Our Life*, London: Eyre & Spottiswoode.

Duck, S. (1980) 'With a Little Help From My Friends', *New Society*, 30.10.80.

—— (1983) *Friends, for Life*, Brighton: Harvester Press.

Fischer, C. (1981) 'Making Friends in the City', *New Society*, 20.8.81.

Gavron, H., (1966) *The Captive Wife*, London: Penguin.

Goldthorpe, J., Lockwood, D., Bechofer, F., and Platt, J., (1969) *The Affluent Worker in Industrial Society*, Cambridge: CUP.

Griffin, C. (1985) *Typical Girls?: Young Women from School to the Job Market*, London: Routledge & Kegan Paul.

Heath, A. (1981) *Social Mobility*, London: Fontana.

McRobbie, A. and Garber, J. (1973) 'Girls and subculture – an exploration', in Hall, S. and Jefferson, T. (eds) *Resistance Through Ritual*, London: Hutchinson.

Morse, S. J. and Marks, A. (1985) 'Cause Duncan's Me Mate – a Comparison of Reported Relations with Mates and Friends in Australia', *British Journal of Social Psychology* 24, November 1985.

Oakley, A. (1975) *Housewife*, London: Allen Lane.

Orbach, S., and Eichenbaum, L. (1987) *Bittersweet*, London: Hutchinson.

Schofield, M. (1965) *The Sexual Behaviour of Young People*, London: Penguin.

Stacy, M. *et al.* (1975) *Power, Persistence and Change: A Second Study of Banbury*, London: Routledge & Kegan Paul.

Steinberg, J. (1981) 'Old Friends, New Times', *New Society*, 20.8.81.

Tunstall, J. (1962) *The Fisherman*, London: MacGibbon & Kee.

Willis, P. (1977) *Learning to Labour*, Westmead: Saxon House.

Willmott, P. (1987) *Friendship Networks and Social Support*, London: Policy Studies Institute.

Young, M., and Willmott, P. (1962) *Family and Kinship in East London*, London: Penguin.

Chapter Nine

FREUD, FRIENDSHIP, AND POLITICS

GRAHAM LITTLE

Friendship came to my notice as a social and political category in interviews my students conducted. The most creative young men and women, and the closest politically to the tradition of philosophical anarchism – they were anti-leader, anti-structure, ultra-participant and as 'fluid' in their politics as in their lifestyles – claimed to live for and through their friendships. The structure they fundamentally opposed was the family, and the only 'leadership' they could countenance was the un-authoritarian leadership of talent, urbanity, and wit. (They liked Trudeau, Whitlam, JFK, up to a point, though they liked more the idea of leadership rotating according to task and circumstance.)

The Ancients, of course, immediately came to mind, Plato and Aristotle[1] pre-eminently, because there was a regular association between creativity, intelligence and living-in- friendships – beyond family, and as gadflies against the State. With 'communion' (as Aristotle called it) went political idealism, and the rejection of mundane social relations. Then there was Montaigne[2], showing how friendship invigorates even when it is short-lived and essentially 'spiritual'; and Francis Bacon[3], plotting a political career out of friendships, now sharply self-aware, now rapturously un-calculating. Eventually, that Edwardian favourite, the dining club, along with the continuing fascination with Bloomsbury – a club with invisible rules, intellectual and sexual at the same time (the combination that makes for being *avant garde*) – took me to St Augustine and the Christian monasteries and then to Kierkegaard[4]. These had to reconcile the egalitarianism of friendships with a third party, God Himself, fashioning a Christian accommodation to the Ancient humanism. A good deal of modern politics – its reassertion of leadership, institutions, the rights of 'society' (the Durkheimian replacement for God) – can be interpreted as anti-friendship, the latter too unorganized, too whimsical, too attached to ideas, innovation and the future for a stable social life. And the climate of opinion is against 'middle-way' parties and those, like the German Greens, 'out-in-front'.

The influence of Durkheim and Marx, both inventors of intellectual juggernauts, on the social sciences left friendship – where the individual and social are delicately poised – with nowhere to go. Some brave attempts, especially Simmel[5] on the dyad and Tarde[6], vainly arguing the case for the salon and the artist against Durkheim's implicit model of the Ministry of Education and the clerks, went largely unnoticed. There was also Schmalenbach[7], a student of Tönnies, who discovered that in religious experience 'church' and 'sect' (secondary group/primary group) did not cover the whole field, and even missed the essential thing, i.e. 'communion': men and women connected with God, like my Australian interviewees in secular terms, in an unmediated way. There are some fascinating essays by anthropologists trying to break out of their systemic harness (fashioned, I suppose chiefly, by Radcliffe Brown): could not there be some give in the system, some room for, paradoxical though this sounds, sociable individuality[8]? The 'institution' of *compadre* appears to have made an opening for theorists of 'primitive' friendship. This was a bastardized Catholic godparent arrangement grafted on to South American Indian traditions, and though it looked like an extension of parental power over, and responsibility for, children, apparently 'godparents' turned into friends (while the children played elsewhere, presumably, as at an Australian barbecue). These – quite outside the kinship and political systems – met, played, exchanged experiences, and recognized and amplified their individual 'identities'.

I began to form an impression of what was distinctive about friendship. Free-play was one thing, i.e. friendship escaped the rules, customs and pieties of social life. Another was that friendship was about identity, i.e. 'who one was' as opposed to one's status and role. And, thirdly, friendship was about hope, the future, the ideas and ideals and larger-than-life meanings people wanted to give their lives. Roles and statuses were derived from institutional and social 'necessities'; the 'idealism' of friendship lies in its detachment from these, its creative and spiritual transcendence, its fundamental scepticism as a platform from which to survey the givens of society and culture.

Other things went with these three critical characteristics, above all egalitarianism. Friends who become too dependent become like children or the poor, objects of compassion more than interest; and a friend who rules the other becomes a kind of parent or older sibling. Friendships require that both parties have self-confidence, that both have the resources to be interesting and hopeful, ideally that each is possessed of creative powers he/she is eager to compare, share, and somehow realize. Also implied is the dyad. Group experience, even in smallish, informal groups ('sects') is something different, demanding some loss of individuality. The self-becoming-the-other, two-becoming-one, and the paradoxical sense that you can be more fully yourself with a friend (a unity that produces diversity), roots friendship in the dyad, the one-to-one encounter. (There are ways in which this becomes not a literal requirement, but something more complex; e.g. some political leaders are experienced one-to-one, though they are literally distant and address mass audiences; and television profits from the illusion of intimacy even as it is the most mass-based medium of all time.)

Durkheim and Marx had little room for paradox, although Marxism was for a time ironic. Happily Victor Turner[9], his anthropology influenced by aesthetic considerations, could make something of friendship where grosser systems could not. Turner first wrote of 'liminal' social occasions, reinvigorating the concept of *rites de passage*. But this only made 'threshold' experiences inverse copies of the social relations that prevailed the rest of the time: the poor became – in manic, festive and temporary defiance – rich, the powerless powerful, and so on. With the 'liminoid', Turner took a further step. In modern societies, satire, parody, lived 'alternatives', are always there, a continuing commentary on the quotidian and the ruling order. In theatre, 'lifestyles', and a variety of social enclaves acting as crucibles for change, criticism and innovation, ritual topsy-turveydom became a permanent shadow play – another, freer, more innovative society, which combined sociability with self-enhancement, or at least claimed to. Profoundly social in encouraging a one-to-one-like 'communion' far removed from bourgeois individualism, liminoid life is also profoundly concerned with singular identities.

Turner, clearly influenced by the Western cultural experience of the sixties, brought friendship – the sceptical, change-oriented (or change-infatuated?), free-flowing form of social relation, where self waxes *with* other – into, shall I say, contention as a distinctive social form. My interest now was in what psychoanalysis could contribute. Was it not, after all, the discipline of thought most sensitive to the threshold on which the individual and society fought, merged or coupled? 'Coupling', as it turned out, proved to be virtually the royal road to the psychoanalytic contribution.

Friendship barely appears in Freud's own writings, and by implication it is inferior to other, grander passions. The key idea is in fact passion restrained; 'friendly relations' are what the sons are reduced to under the authority of the primal father in Freud's guiding myth of the origins of civilization, set out in *Totem and Taboo* and in *Group Psychology and The Analysis of the Ego*. Friends are first sons, then equals, their quality a derivative of their coinciding ties to the leader. Two things are involved here. One is, I think, an analytic and sceptical habit of mind which is hostile to paradox. The other, of which I am more sure, is Freud's concern with aggressiveness, his belief that desire always involves rivalry, that human passions are ambivalent because they are always entangled with authority relations on the model of father-son desire and rivalry. Montaigne's 'him who is not another but is myself' – echoed in my students' interviews – would have seemed to Freud a regressive idea, an obvious illusion in which men (especially) take refuge from earthy Oedipal desire and rivalry in idealism: in ideas, in a spotless, utopian futurism, in unbridled (and un-'generative') creativity. There is a hint of narcissism: Montaigne's friend, La Boétie, is, after all, long dead and only a character in Montaigne's written life – is he perhaps absorbed and recycled, rather than known and allowed his own life?[10] Also, for all its claim to uncommon vitality, this 'communion' of friends has a taint of death like the figures on Keats' Grecian Urn. Theirs is a unity of souls joined in an unchanging, silent harmony, not of men contracting with each other, exchanging, sometimes agreeing, sometimes challenging. In such harmony, otherness and life are lost.

Yet Freud himself knew a great deal about friendship, and his work was nurtured by it more than by any other kind of relationship. 'Passion', writes Marthe Robert[11], 'is not too strong' a word to describe Freud's 'extraordinary attachment' to his friend Fliess. One letter, 'one of many like it', runs:

> People like you should not die out my dear friend; we others need the likes of you too much. How much have I to thank you for in consolation, understanding, stimulation in my loneliness, in the meaning of life you have given me. . . it is essentially your example that has enabled me to gain the intellectual strength to trust my own judgement. . . .
>
> (Robert 1966: 89)

There were numerous friends in his youth – chief among them being Heinrich Braun, a journalist – sounding-boards for Freud's ideas, and mirrors in which he could fashion his developing identity. This continued throughout his life, where Freud showed a strong inclination to band his friends and supporters together, issuing rings and instituting oaths of loyalty, though Robert reminds us that some friends could count on Freud's loyalty even though they refused to be his followers, including Oscar Pfister, who was and remained a Protestant clergyman.

Nevertheless, two features of Freud's friendships – or the one feature viewed from two different angles – are of a piece with the neglect of friendship in his theorizing. One was that they had to end, and did so acrimoniously; the other was that they tended to be unequal. There was, in other words, a fundamental ambivalence in which a 'brother transference' – an equal partnership – was associated with a 'father transference' which would eventually take over, so that the friend/father had to be repudiated. 'Freud, it seems, needed to be indebted to his friends in some way. . .' (even, as a young man, materially): he 'had to love and admire a man who was both close to him and superior to him, from whom he expected not only support and affectionate help, but a kind of inspiration, an example that would stimulate him'. And McGrath[12], tracing the links between Freud's youthful political ambitions – his Hannibal fantasy and his identification with rebels against authority – shows Freud deeply attracted to the band of brothers, 'young lions', whose passionate, egalitarian solidarity had as its *raison d'être* a challenge to the 'fathers'.

147

The most written about and illuminating friendship was with Fliess. There is no mistaking in their correspondence the importance Freud placed on this friendship, which replaced the one with Breuer[13]:

> When I talked to you, and thought that you thought
> something of me, I actually started thinking something of
> myself. . .
> After each of our congresses I have been newly fortified for
> weeks, new ideas press forward, pleasure in the hard work was
> restored, the flickering hope of finding one's way through the
> jungle burned for a while steadily and brightly. . .
> I can write nothing if I have no public at all, but I am perfectly
> content to write only for you.
>
> (Robert 1966: 91)

We can look at this friendship as we did before, and as Freud did later: 'I *no longer* have any need to uncover my personality completely. . . Since Fliess's case. . .that need has been extinguished. A part of homosexual cathexis has been withdrawn and made use of to enlarge my own ego. I have succeeded where the paranoic fails'[14]; i.e., we could interpret friendship as essentially the displacement of love and hate for the father, and as such a developmental arrest that needs to be overcome if a man is to realize his powers.

But Heinz Kohut, the only psychoanalytic theorist I know who has explicitly made a place for friendship in his theory[15], reads it in a different way. Kohut reminds us that Freud's friendship with Fliess was at its most intense during the great self-analysis that led to *The Interpretation of Dreams* and to psychoanalysis itself. He reads Freud's idealization of Fliess and his basking in his (putative) approval as a necessary adjunct to the 'de-construction' Freud was going through. Fliess's very ordinariness, solid and uncritical, was just what nascent genius required. In Kohut's terms, Fliess was a 'self-object' – not a conspiratorial brother, not a 'good' father, but a person on whom to rely for one's fundamental sense of being and in whom to see one's emerging self as it took shape. Self-objects are not parent figures. At least, they are parents in another (pre-Oedipal) sense: experienced as soothing and responsive at a time when the boundaries between self and other (child and parent) are fluid, they become absorbed into a core sense of self which, ideally, is cohesive and permeated with a sense of agency. The developmental outcome of early self-object relations is selfhood itself.

This was particularly evident in my students' interviews with youthful, creative individuals, the friend as a guarantor of identity. You will notice too how similar it is to the description I gave earlier of friendship's distinctive elements: experiment or free play; identity; the future. Friendship can mean neighbourliness and it can mean the experience of comrades-in-arms, but these may be readily understood psychoanalytically as extensions of family relations, of motherly love and fatherly protection. In a 'strong' sense, 'friendship' is additional or instead of these, and its focus is not distinctively on caring or working together but on exchanges of self-knowledge – on confirmation of existence, and the building up of hopes of what one will, ideally, amount to as a singular person.

Kohut's theory goes on to link friendships with wit, wisdom and creativity. He sees it flourishing when overarching 'identities' are fragmented, as in times of rapid cultural exchange, or in turning points in individual lives. And he links it with lives lived at odds with social prescriptions and eager to develop further throughout adulthood. Self-objects – parodied, it must be admitted, in flatterers and the fashion for 'stroking', rigidified in groups which aim to promote psychological 'growth' therapeutically, etc. – continue to be necessary and fruitful throughout adult life, as a social oxygen that maintains a sense of being a person among other persons.

There is a portability about friendship (and self-objects) which allows the individual who is uprooted, déclassé, sophisticated and urbane, to feel continuously confirmed though the social setting changes. Kohut's theory has the feel of 'other-directed' America, influenced no doubt by his own translation from Vienna to Chicago; it is certainly some kind of answer – transposing 'self-object' into 'friendship' – to Durkheim's 'anomie' and Marx's 'alienation'. But British psychoanalysts have been playing with similar ideas, formulating an approach of their own. The starting point here is the increasingly influential 'Independent Tradition'[16] and, pre-eminently, D.W. Winnicott.

The 'British School' can be credited with shifting emphasis from the Oedipal triangle, where all is urgent desire and intense rivalry (and at best, friendship is the comradeship of soldiers, workmates and footballers) to the two-person dilemma of 'separation', child from mother. But 'friendship' in this view – though, once again, the concept is unfocused in the theories – subsides into communal or neighbourly feeling, into 'primary group' loyalties and political and social solidarities with the feel of religious communities. This is often what the Left, opposing the thinness of social relations on the Right, proposes as friendship. In the Kleinian tradition, to separate is good, but to be thankful is better; maturity equals individualism, envy and rivalry, held in check by grateful co-operation. As with Freud there is a dualism, though here the emphasis is not on 'enlarging the ego' separately but on paying one's debts to the nurturers, familial and social, on leaving but then 'coming home' (like the Prodigal Son).

Winnicott[17] looked for a middle way, and opted boldly for paradox. The 'transitional object' (the teddy bear) *can* be a way of holding on so that no separating, no individualizing, takes place. But, to the extent that it really is transitional, it becomes a bridge over which the child will travel to and fro. The transitional object is partly mother and the past, but partly too a creation of one's own, and a sign of the future. Relations between people also can be transitional. To speak of *my* friend is to sound defensive and consuming, afraid to let go; my *friend*, however, can co-exist with this, so that you and I are, at our best, simultaneously intertwined and singular. Winnicott aphoristically sums up his view of individual maturity as 'the capacity to be alone in the presence of another'. He links this capacity with the wish and capacity to absorb what is handed on culturally while feeling free to create; not impression or expression, but both. He sees civilized life as being ideally a 'potential space' – a place in-between (shades of Turner's liminoid) where the traffic is both ways, from self to other, from other to self.

It is difficult to do justice to these newer psychoanalytic theories in a short space, and I am not quite finished. I hope enough has been said – and I have referred only to the most obvious, well-used ideas – to indicate how relevant contemporary psychoanalysis is for the study of friendship. It is important to remember that these ideas originated in clinical and development studies, are constantly referred back there, and that they have their roots in unconscious processes. All too easily, talk of friendship is restricted to aphorism and anecdote, or is merely wishful thinking, a matter of facile paradox and convenient 'middle ways'. These ideas may be wrong. But at least they are part of a tradition of thought in which rivals to friendship – above all the hotbed of family relations – and rival interpretations are well-entrenched and likely to keep the romance of one-to-one, 'authentic' relations more or less honest[18].

Indeed the last theorist I want to mention is Wilfred Bion, known best for his *Experiences In Groups,* who shows how deeply fantasy penetrates the idea of friendship. Bion saw groups revolving through three, unconsciously-driven, positions. In one, 'Dependency', relations are community-like, solidary, uncreative. In another, 'Fight-Flight', the group structures itself for decisive action, in retreat or attack, and the concern is not love but survival. The third position brings us to friendship as coupling. As Bion[19] describes it,

> two members of the group would become involved in a discussion;. . .it would be evident that they were involved with each other. . . On these occasions the group would sit in attentive silence. . . Whenever two people begin to have this kind of relationship in a group – whether these two are man and woman, man and man or woman and woman – it seems to be a basic assumption, held both by the group and the pair concerned, that the relationship is a sexual one. . . .
>
> It usually finds expression verbally in ideas that marriage would put an end to neurotic disabilities, that group therapy would revolutionise society. . .that the coming season. . .will be more agreeable – that some kind of community – an improved group – should be developed, and so on. These expressions tend to divert attention to some supposedly future event but. . . the crux is not a future event but the immediate present – the feeling of hope itself.
>
> (Little 1985: 81, 88)

The dyad, intelligence and creativity, the future, the whole romance of friendship are all present here. My students' interviews, though individual character studies, almost exactly reproduce these features: inspiring leaders 'pair' with their ecstatic followers; the leaders 'pair' with wives or colleagues (the Kennedys and the Gorbachevs); they are idealistic, change-oriented, clever, far more urbane than ordinary mortals

(Trudeau), etc. etc. This fantasy of coupling is the template of friendship – a template built out of hope, drawn, in Bion's reading, from the child's rapt impression of its parents' sexual/emotional coupling. Thus groups revolve from mother to father then to mother and father together, and its members feel predominantly safe and snug, or bold and determined, or (as in friendship) youthfully creative, forward-looking and united effortlessly in their excitement and hope about an ideal.

The great value of Bion's observation on pairing, and the view of friendship as coupling, is that one need neither glorify friendship at the expense of familial or contractual relations, nor derogate it for its romantic idealism. All the group positions are driven by fantasies – of merger with mother, of acquiring patriarchal powers, of reproducing the parental embrace – but all yield, with work, a portion of human experience and social life: family-like relations, work-like relations, friendship. The significance for friendship as a focus of social and political interest is not that it is a solution, a synthetic answer to the great oppositions of social thought, but simply that it is allowed to exist on the psychosocial map. Where Freud bequeathes us only suspicion in approaching the 'communion' of Aristotle or Schmalenbach (and their equivalents in other theories), Bion, yielding pre-eminence neither to Hobbes nor Rousseau, lets us examine friendship's claims open-mindedly. He refuses it the whole field but, admitting its roots in fantasy, he gives it a reality it has lacked.

One last thing is the patient-analyst relation itself. Psychoanalysis, like any other discourse, is subject to being routinized. Ironically, given Freud's hostility to religion, it can at the same time turn into a sect. Recently, however, there has been a revival of interest in characterizing the psychoanalytic relation, and the accompanying moves to reform (though practice was frequently ahead of theory or dogma) have been in the direction of rediscovering the pure dyad, and the creative-cum-sceptical asceticism one associates with truth-seeking more than therapeutics. Lacan has had an important influence here. Bion called for the removal of 'memory and desire'[20], suggesting pure interaction rather as Simmel described the dyad. Kohut too believed he could start each session anew, and Winnicott, in a moving account of his early experiences as an analyst[21], explains how the concept of 'holding' – where nothing was said and the previously harried patient slept – prefigured his idea that sociability could include presence without intrusion. (My students' interviewees were proud that they had friends with whom they could take up immediately, after long absences, and thought a good friend was one whom you could leave – 'to have a sleep', one said – when you needed to be alone.)

All of these suggest a relationship which, though contractural and unequal in part, and though helping and compassionate in part, is distinctively one-to-one, intellectually without boundaries (legal, pious and even logical), intent on defusing without disowning the past and, ranging back and forth, aimed at the future. There is extreme consciousness and blundering unconsciousness, intimacy and distance, absence and presence, intense identification and ultimate autonomy. The claims of friendship may be utopian. Nevertheless, in psychoanalysis, buttressed by more ordinary social arrangements (unfortunately mostly those of the western middle class) it can be rehearsed. It would be surprising if psychoanalytic theory had nothing to say about friendship when everything it knows is drawn from a relationship which so closely resembles it.

Some closing questions: is friendship – in this 'strong' sense – open more to men than women? Freud implied yes; Bion's 'pairing' group position is androgynous. Indeed, though young 'aesthetic' males form one cluster in our interviews, there is another comprising women whose marriages have ended, who are in search of a more singular but not isolated existence. These speak of a friend who offered 'holding' while they rearranged their lives. Unlike families, who may support well but are uncomfortable with an individual's changing, and unlike workmates, who want the changes dealt with quickly, a friend 'holds' you while you change. Is friendship age-specific? The men are young, the women older. This may be related to different developmental timetables, or to social demands, such as the mothering role; but do post-parental men turn to soul mates? Is friendship for turning points only, for certain classes (the new aristocracy of the educated, or those well-placed to change jobs and marriage partners at mid-life)? Is friendship something that can become virtually a visible section of society – the liminoid sector comprising artists, writers, Arts intellectuals – or can it be an 'invisible' accompaniment to other social relations, subtly relativizing them? How is friendship related to sex? Freud took it to be an expression of people's bisexuality, so that friendship depended on homosexuality; Bion's 'pairing' group position is indifferent to sex: the couple can be of the same sex or of the opposite but they must not actually pair off.

There is a host of further questions. But what of politics? There are utopian suggestions that friendship – the exchange of identities and ideals, egalitarian and 'fluid' exchanges, stimulation to radical criticism and original ideas – could be, by itself, the shape of a new society. Unfortunately, the direction of this idea is towards the shallowness and self-absorption of Southern California. I doubt that Romanticism's 'affinities' can be the whole of social life. Bloomsbury itself is a clear warning of how inadequately friendship handles either the raising of children or the performance of public duties; Keynes, it will be remembered, upset his fellow members by being so willing to do public service and by being so good at it. However, the larger formations of social life – kinship, the law, the economy – must be different where there is, in addition to solidarity and dutiful role-performance, a willingness and capacity for friendship's surprising one-to-one relations, and this difference may be enough to transform social and political life.

In any biography, friendship is likely to be overlooked in favour of family, lovers, colleagues and rivals; the lone genius needs re-inspection – he may be a man or a woman with an invisible soul-mate. Political leaders might be judged in part on the experience of friendship. Nye Bevan, for example, built his political identity in days and nights of youthful talk – Freud/Fliess-like? – with a friend who stayed with him until Bevan's death, and there were many more friends, not all 'Bevanites'. A profound, non-bourgeois individualism, an escape from mere economic man, would seem likelier and more believable where the leader has known what friendship is. Margaret Thatcher, as an example of the opposite, has had many colleagues and helpers and works in a fiercely loyal team but there is little evidence of her having a friend or two – alter-egos, mirrors, guides – or that in childhood and adolescence there were friendships that took her out of her social loyalties and fixed ideas into something more critical, inventive and authentically personal.

Perhaps, finally, it is true that progress in democracy depends on a new generation that will increasingly locate itself in identity-shaping, social, yet personally liberating, friendships. The family is still the chief model for political relations, much of politics a struggle between the authority of father and the authority of mother, directive, secret and excluding[22]. Freud saw the children, the siblings, as unable to do more than react to this, but then he understood American democracy hardly at all. Later psychoanalytic ideas encourage us to take friendship seriously, seeing it as a mix of fantasy and reality but admitting the positive sibling relations. Children's friendships, grown into adult readiness for involved, equal partnership, may yet enhance the chances for a democracy increasingly built on sociable individuals[23].

NOTES

1 David Bolotin (1979) *Plato's Dialogue on Friendship: An Interpretation of the* 'Lysis', *with a new translation*, Ithaca: Cornell University Press, provides a graceful and stimulating reading of Plato on friendship. Jeffrey B. Abramson (1984) *Liberation And Its Limits: The Moral and Political Thought of Freud*, New York: Free Press, makes Aristotle and friendship the centrepiece of his criticism of Freud's 'Hobbesianism'. Two stimulating philosophical articles, relating friendship and the Ancients, are: Michael Stocker (1981) 'Values and Purposes: The Limits of Teleology and the Ends of Friendship', *The Journal of Philosophy* 78, no. 12, Dec. 1981: 747–65 and Ferdinand Schoeman (1985) 'Aristotle on the Good of Friendship', *Australasian Journal of Philosophy* 63, no. 3, September 1985: 269–82.

2 (1958) *Essays*, Harmondsworth: Penguin Books. I am inclined to ignore that stream of research on friendship which treats it as a technique. See, for example, Steven Duck (1977) *The Study of Acquaintance*, Farnborough: Saxon House, which uses Kelley's 'personal constructs' theory.

3 *Francis Bacon's Essays*, introduction by Oliver Smeaton, London: J. M. Dent (Everyman's Library), 1906 (1958), essay twenty-seven. Bacon's essay includes the felicitous phrase 'this communicating of a man's self to his friend', a phrase that points to the centrality of 'identity' concerns in friendship and to language. The latter, as I find in interviews, is a *sine qua non* of 'strong' friendship. Curiously, an early English explorer of Australia, Matthew Flinders, gives an active man's support to the idea that friendship is about shared identities: 'It is the almost indescribable communion of mind, the similarity of sentiments and of taste, and that jumping together of the heart' – with esteem and care – that 'are the foundations of ardent genuine friendship. . .', from Sydney J. Baker (1962) *My Own Destroyer, A*

Biography of Matthew Flinders, Explorer and Navigator, Sydney: Currawong Publishing Co., p. 92.

4 Kierkegaard's friendship with Emil Boesen, lasting from childhood to death, is shaded by the worry that God would be forgotten. To his 'comrade' and 'good presence', Kierkegaard writes, 'You know how I am, how in conversation with you I jump about stark naked, whereas I am always enormously calculating with other people' – but their shared motto was 'A Church stands in the distance'. See J. Collins (1981) 'Kierkegaard's Imagery of the Self' in J. H. Smith (ed.) *Kierkegaard's Truth: The Disclosure of the Self*, New Haven: Psychiatry and the Humanities, vol. 5, Yale University Press.

5 Georg Simmel (1971) *On Individuality and Social Forms* (ed. D. N. Levine), Chicago: Chicago University Press, especially the essay 'Sociability'. My own *Political Ensembles: A Psychosocial Approach to Leadership and Politics*, Melbourne: Oxford University Press, 1985, chapter two, has a more extended treatment of the ideas here, including remarks on Schmalenbach, Tarde, Turner and Simmel, and on friendship itself.

6 Stephen Lukes (1975) *Emile Durkheim, His Life and Work*, Harmondsworth: Penguin Books, describes the debate between Tarde and Durkheim and it appears more or less in full in Gabriel Tarde (1969) *On Communication and Social Influence*, Chicago: Chicago University Press, chapter four. Tarde's high estimation of the importance of conversation in social life links with my students' interviewees' inclination to make friendship and talk almost synonymous.

7 Hermann Schmalenbach (1977) *On Society and Experience* (translated and edited by G. Luschen and G. P. Stone), Chicago: Chicago University Press. Schmalenbach pinpoints the paradoxical character of friendship, its boundary-crossing: e.g. 'emotional experiences are the very stuff of the relationships' yet its substance 'is actually the cognitive recognition of feeling'. Intensity *and* awareness are both sought.

8 S. N. Eisenstadt (1956) 'Ritualized Personal Relations', *Man*, Vol. 5, pp. 90–5 stands at the pole where friendship is only strain in the system. Y. A. Cohen (1964) 'Patterns of Friendship', in Y. A. Cohen (ed.) *Social Structure and Personality: A Casebook*, New York: Holt, Rinehart and Winston, pulls away from this. In a modern context the case against Eisenstadt is taken up by Robert Paine (1969), 'In search of friendship: an exploratory analysis in 'middle-class' culture', *Man*, New Series Vol. 4, no. 4, pp. 505–24. The argument seems to hinge on whether the ambiguity and lability of friendship, hard to capture in structural-functionalist schemes, rules it out as a genuine 'social' phenomenon. Does 'society' begin only with the third term?

9 See especially Victor Turner (1979) *Process, Performance and Pilgrimage: A Study in Comparative Symbology*, New Delhi: Concept Publishing Co., and (1977) *The Ritual Process*, Ithaca: Cornell University Press. As the first title suggests, Turner's view of social life is at odds with that of the

doyenne of social anthropology, Mary Douglas, whose 'Grid' and 'Group' only reluctantly yield a little space for 'un-anchored' and 'over-personalized' relations like friendship.

10 The paradox in friendship – its simultaneous attention to self and to other (which, empirically, may be a rare feat) – is not recognized in Floyd Gray's treatment of Montaigne ('Montaigne's Friends', *French Studies*, Vol. 15, no. 3, July 1961). He sees Montaigne as 'self-centred' and 'bookish', merely 'essaying friendship' rather than describing it (or actually experiencing it). This is where the newer psychoanalytic ideas come in: a psychoanalysis of the self, including the relationships in which selfhood, or identity, develops, can drive the paradox deeper if not finally resolve it.

11 Marthe Robert (1966) *The Psychoanalytic Revolution, Sigmund Freud's Life and Achievement*, London: George Allen & Unwin. The following quotations are from p. 90 and p. 89 respectively.

12 William J. McGrath (1986) *Freud's Discovery of Psychoanalysis: The Politics of Hysteria*, Ithaca: Cornell University Press, makes a powerful case for the role of friendship in Freud's early achievements, though on the whole he leans more on the 'father-complex' than the 'brother' one.

13 Marthe Robert (1966), p. 91.

14 Marthe Robert (1966), p. 246.

15 Though explicitly only, in his posthumous (1984) *How Does Analysis Cure?* (ed. by Arnold Goldberg, with the collaboration of Paul E. Stepansky), Chicago: Chicago University Press, p. 201 – and there his examples are not quite good enough. But the general idea *is* good: that human beings need throughout their lives a sense of the presence of other human beings – a sense of person-to-person potentiality – if their own selfhood is to remain intact and even expand. For Kohut's view of the Freud-Fliess 'self-object transference' see (1978) *The Search For The Self* (ed. by P. Ornstein), New York: International Universities Press, Vol. 2, chapter 48: 'Creativeness, Charisma, Group Psychology: Reflections on the Self-Analysis of Freud'.

16 Gregorio Kohon (1986) *The British School of Psychoanalysis: The Independent Tradition*, London: Free Association Books begins with a now well-known article by Christopher Bollas 'The Transformational Object' in which, for example, to quote Kohon, 'the first object – the mother – [is] not so much. . .an object. . .as a *process* of alteration of self experience' (p. 76). In her psychoanalytic study of early development Victoria Hamilton (1982) *Narcissus and Oedipus: The Children of Psychoanalysis*, London: Routledge & Kegan Paul, argues richly for 'interactional synchrony and mutuality' as the child's starting point. Work reported by Virginia Demos, in Boston, which involves the close study of affective exchanges between mother and child similarly strengthens the 'interactional' case – which in turn takes friendship, rule-less and reliant on moment-by-moment success in communicating, close to the heart of human sociability. (See, for example, Virginia Demos (1983) 'A Perspective From Infant Research On Affect and Self-Esteem' in J. Mack and S. Ablon, *The Development*

and Sustaining of Self-esteem, New York: International Universities Press.)

17 Winnicott's publications are numerous, but his accessible (1971) *Playing and Reality*, Harmondsworth: Penguin Books, is an ideal starting point, not least the essays 'The Location of Cultural Experience' and 'The Place Where We Live'.

18 Out of ignorance I have slighted Jacques Lacan, but even more so Carl Jung whose animus/anima has obviously strong links with the Ancients, e.g. Aristotle's '*alter ego*' version of the friend. Moreover, Jung was for a long time the only 'analytic' theorist of adult development, in which now Kohut and others insist friendship has important functions.

19 Quoted in Little (1985) *Political Ensembles*, pp. 81, 88.

20 F. Bion (1980) *Bion in New York and Sao Paulo*, Perthshire: Clunie Press. In these recorded discussions Bion is at his most cryptic, not to say gnomic. 'The biological unit', he remarks in New York, 'is a couple' – echoing in a very different context R. Brain's discovery of an African tribe whose cosmology is based on the belief that each person is one half of a twin, the other half to be sought among visiting strangers ((1976) *Friends and Lovers*, London: Paladin).

21 D. W. Winnicott (1986) *Holding and Interpretation, Fragment of an Analysis*, London: The Hogarth Press. In Kohut, more than in Winnicott, the emphasis in psychoanalytic practice is on empathy, not sympathy or knowledge, but the general direction is similar – and 'empathy' seems the *mot juste* for friendship.

22 The Society of Friends showed the way in England's political history. Here is George Fox to his parents, recommending that they follow *his* example on the 'inner light', or fully subjective authenticity, a politics of 'authenticity': 'Dear Father and Mother in the flesh, but not to that birth which speaks to you. . .praises be given to my heavenly Father, who hath begotten me again by the immortal word. . .' Hugh Barbour and Arthur Roberts (eds) (1973) *Early Quaker Writings*, Grand Rapids: W. E. Erdmans, p. 48.

23 My (1985) *Political Ensembles* uses the idea of 'ensemble' to characterize social relations – humanly social relations – not derived from and critically distinct from those relations shaped by contract (Structure) and kinship-like sentiment (Group). Ensemble relations can be *all* that a person wants or is capable of, useful like charismatic leader-follower relations, for creativity, criticism and change, but unreliable in more quotidian pursuits. Similarly, there can be a utopian pursuit of friendship ('authentic relationships'?) or an infusion of friendship's distinctive qualities into other kinds of relations, in families and neighbourhoods, at work, in politics, etc. The Group, the Left's answer to anomie and alienation, needs friendship as much as Structure does, or the individual suffocates – or leaves.

Chapter Ten

THE ENVIRONMENT OF FELLOWSHIP AROUND 1900

LOGIE BARROW

'Fellowship is life, lack of fellowship is death' proclaimed William Morris during 1886, some years into his final, revolutionary marxist phase. During the period around 1900, a heretical middle-class discussion about friendship found complicated echoes from some people whose own, mostly humbler, milieux had rather different traditions. Both these currents were heretical in relation to an increasingly assertive, indeed pervasive, propaganda about 'manliness'. 'Heretical' is, though, a distinct exaggeration as compared with the situation of those – male homosexuals notably – who were subjected to moral panic on a scale unprecedented during at least the nineteenth century: explicitly or not, it was they who called 'manliness' into question. These were the full heretics. Few others identified with them, at least openly. Rather the milder rebels – both middle and working class – were identifiable via their political involvements. In this sphere, their thinking on friendship blurred with questions which have helped confuse generations of more or less left-wing political activists: as to how to relate individual to social emancipation.

This blurring helped give currency to at least three types of friendly relationship: the small, earnestly philosophical group; the large and loose grouping characterized by occasional in-joking and by vague satire on the rituals of more formal organizations (such as Freemasons, unions or friendly societies); and a far smaller and, so far as can be traced, rarer type of group which nurtured satire and in-joking as against virtually everything else.

From the early 1880s – i.e. from a few years before Morris's monthly *Commonweal* printed our opening motto – the 'Fellowship of the New Life' set out to change the world by philosophical

159

means. It remained tiny and close, though never tight, and survived fitfully for more than a decade[1]. Historians have tended to consign it to the dustbin of history – yet some of the ingredients of this dustbin were constantly being recycled at great speed. In the context of strivings for and about friendship, this fellowship was scarcely more than an organizational sprout within a compost of influences such as those of Ruskin, the pre-Raphaelites (Morris, of course, most durably), Emerson, Thoreau, Whitman, Tolstoy, 'Krapotkine' (as he was then often transliterated) and Edward Carpenter. These and other writers were read as aiming to regenerate society by regenerating each individual – a process which required thoroughly authentic relationships between individuals and with nature. They conceived the latter unproblematically and – Darwin or no – optimistically. Their dilemmas about the relation between individual and social regeneration were often couched in language which, to them, felt new. In substance, though, their concepts of political strategy represented little if any advance on those of earlier British socialists, notably Robert Owen and the Owenites half a century or more previously. Usually, the difference was merely one of jargon: Owen had agonized over environmental determination of character, whereas the *circa* 1900 reformers talked a plurality of jargons. But the substance had hardly changed.

In effect, some 1890s activists outdid the Owenites, as far as the setting up of communes ('communities') was concerned. These were mostly rural, in locations as various as Croydon and Paraguay (just as Owenites had tried to settle in places as various as Hampshire and Indiana). On paper, these might have appeared to some contemporaries to be pregnant with possibilities of new rhythms of friendship. But – to take the most notorious of these possibilities – heretical views on marriage were much weaker amongst 1890s left-wingers than they had been amongst the Owenites[2]. And anyway, few of the 1890s collectivist colonies enjoyed long or happy lives. Thus, except when their dissensions reached the radical press, they placed themselves on the margin of any discussion of friendship.

It was in print, early in the 1900s, that Owenism was revived – though as a doctrine, and without much mention of Owen. This was done by Robert Blatchford, a former regular army sergeant who had founded and now blew the *Clarion*, the most successful socialist weekly during the period, and the one which tried most to link personal to political emancipation. For Owen, socialism had been 'the Social system'; for the *Clarion*, education and sociability or 'Fellowship' became the key to political emancipation[3].

Talk of the *Clarion* and of the press would bring us from our first (philosophical) type of friendship to our second. But here we must place, likewise on the margin, one particularly important grouping: had the Fabians not originated (1884) in a secession from the New Lifers, the latter would have been even more forgotten than they have been.

Historians[4] have agreed with leading Fabians that the Society catered peculiarly for a 'new social layer' of higher clerical employees, junior professionals, civil servants and would-be intellectuals. True, for a very few years around 1890, the Society also had an organized provincial following who were more plebeian and often even more variegated in origin and in political trajectory. But the point, here, about the metropolitan Fabians is that they were self-consciously metropolitan: close to the levers of power and influence. This prospect could structure the life of even a lowly-born denizen of Whitehall such as Sidney Webb – all the more, once he had allied himself in marriage with Beatrice Potter (who had recently rejected a very likely more conventional alliance with no less than Joseph Chamberlain, already one of the key politicians of her time). That their relationship involved what one of them praised as 'perfect self-deadness' does not mean it was cold, but merely that it was without distractions from its entirely political goal. The Webbs never made any pretence of offering a model for others' relationships – any more than, say, the highly public Bernard Shaw or, later, the promiscuous H. G. Wells ever so pretended.

And this is why we can place leading Fabians in parentheses as far as friendship is concerned. True, the Society continued through many changes and decades to provide a forum for, amongst others, some youngish people of a range of social backgrounds more or less similar to that of the founders. But to the (great) extent that these people were unprepared to adopt Webbian self-deadness, they remained under the influence of old or new ideals of friendship. Self-deadness would perhaps have been one understandable response by a young man or woman to the shocking vastness of late nineteenth-century London. It was certainly an ambitious one politically, but no less a fatalistic one personally and, apparently for most of them, no less unnecessary. By contrast, the Webbs' political ambition was itself directed towards a strategy which Owen – in his naïver fashion – had attempted long before there had been working-class Owenites, and which he occasionally hankered after: that of reforming the social environment by appealing to existing holders of power. What the Webbs and their immediate circle called 'permeation' involved an approach more or less as instrumental as in any other arena where friendship blurs with influence and intrigue.

By contrast, Blatchford's revival of Owenite dilemmas involved a highl conditional attitude to immediate reforms, whether introduced from above or anywhere else: they were desirable only insofar as they assisted in 'educating the people in Socialism'. His Owenism (which he saw as 'my determinism' for its insistence that environment 'determined' character) became famous or infamous with its deterministic onslaught on Christianity and, more relevantly to an anthology on friendship, his no less deterministic defence of the 'bottom dog'. But the whole strategy which the *Clarion* writers laid down for socialism was based on the hope of overcoming the old determinist conundrum which had bedevilled the Owenites throughout: given that environment determined character, how could still-stunted character not undermine an improved environment? This conundrum lay at the doctrinal root of the extraordinarily multifarious interest around the 1890s in socialism as a 'religion'[5]. The *Clarion* at first helped further this interest, but its solution remained always education: at first political education but, from the 1900s, Blatchford also emphasized, as a precondition for this, intellectual liberation from superstition. It was for the sake of political-educational clarity that, more than once, he risked a split in what, at the time, was Britain's least sectarian socialist organization, the Independent Labour Party and, in 1911, actually did help split it.

Determinist strategies had always had an inherent tendency to efface themselves before what were officially no more than their preconditions. In mid-century, very many Owenites had provisionally narrowed their strategy to one of producers' and (far more often) consumers' co-operation. In addition some Owenites and others had, as Blatchford was to do later, despaired of making progress until they had levered off from the minds of the masses the dead weight of superstition. So they came to concentrate on propaganda against religion and to rename themselves 'secularists'. Obviously, Blatchford's own trumpeting of his 'determinism' (which he, in his ignorance, saw as *his*) involved a repeat of this latter effacement. But, throughout his period, he was also involved in a simpler and more practical strategy: encouraging the *Clarion*'s readers to set up Clarion Cycling Clubs (which peaked at 180 or more).

These existed both for 'spreading the [socialist] gospel on wheels' and for promoting something which Blatchford called 'Fellowship' which brings us to our second form of friendship. With less spectacular success, he also promoted, from the 1890s, what he called 'Cinderellas': clubs for providing food with fun for the poorest working-class children and, from around 1900, a 'Clarion Fellowship' as such. But 'as such' is simply too heavy. As Blatchford himself expressed it, 'Socialism is Fellowship, mutual happiness and enjoyment is Fellowship, therefore the Fellowship is for all these things'. More important, 'Fellowship' had in any case been the nearest that any Clarion organizations had to any ideology distinct not only from that of non-socialist organizations (here, the warm indiscrimination of Cinderella activities was seen as a protest against the distrustful moralism of established charities) but also from other socialist organizations: 'the Fellowship', for the individualist-socialist Leonard Hall, meant 'rais[ing] and rous[ing]' socialism from 'Socialist caucus-men, official faking politicals on the make, and ... dreary, damnable impossibilist Calvinism ... chiefly by honest laughter and a sense of proportion'. But these qualities were certainly less definable than those which, say, the New Lifers had sought to cultivate. Fellowship was thus more co-optable politically: indeed 'the' Fellowship was inaugurated at a time when British socialists were at their most depressed – not least by Blatchford's outspoken support for the war in South Africa, a war which symbolized their apparent failure. Yet co-option was not seen as necessarily a danger: more as a spreading of one's ideal. Thus the definition and therefore the limits of *Clarion* influence are hard to define.

'Fellowship', centrally, was also seen as answering another of the determinist conundra: how to prevent the aim becoming abstract. During an earlier generation, those Owenites in particular who had continued to work and live within their existing ('old, immoral') environment had sought to strengthen their system by developing a rich associative life: this was why their system was thus not merely 'new and moral' but, above all, 'social'. Later, they and their successors had been less optimistic about the likely speed of change. The 'Clarionettes' carried this to an extreme. For them, though, there was also the hope of pre-tasting one's ideal.

As one *Clarion* reader sighed:

> the idea is still a long way off and many a weary mile lies between us and the delectable mountains. . . In addition to the faraway paradise, [the *Clarion*] endeavours to help us realize, at least approximately, a little heaven of our own.

Similarly a decade-and-a-half later, Blatchford's aide, A. M. Thompson, remembered the Fellowship's early members as having had

> no explicit end in view, but . . . to provide for some relief from that greyness and dullness against which all socialists are struggling, to establish for themselves immediately some foretaste of that Fellowship which it is the purpose of their strivings to secure eventually for all mankind.

But, around this time, shelter from stormy blasts was sometimes available from gatherings which were not merely more local and therefore usually less recorded, but were also so distinctive as to amount to a third type of friendship. Liverpool's 'Pezzers', i.e. Pessimists, provide the best example. They might have gone unrecorded – after all, their very formation was itself partly a satirical protest against any formality anywhere – but for the printing of their 'founder and perpetual president', R.T. Manson's pictogramically *Wayward Fancies* of 1892–1906. This cosmically materialist and cynically anti-capitalist perpetration was prefaced and officially transcribed by a *Clarion* writer[6]. And the Pezzers certainly included a number of local Clarionettes and other socialists. Manson, a sometime coffeehouse proprietor, led among the Clarionettes. True, 'most' Pezzers are described as 'decent, respectable businessmen of Liverpool and its vicinity'. But our source for this was a socialist stonemason who was himself initiated as a Pezzer around (as it happens) the time of these *Fancies'* publication[7]. And Manson himself was said to 'chortle with glee' whenever, a week or so after a Pezzer's nocturnal midwinter 'razzle', 'he heard . . . that one of the band was down with flu or pneumonia'. This was hardly a fellowly sentiment, however 'pessimistic'. But Manson embodied paradoxes: partly by affecting to believe that 'life was a horrid dream, and . . . death . . . the only thing worth dying for', he himself seems to have remained thoroughly happy and healthy. True again, his long-term philosophy – in which the earth would one day be consumed by fire – was paraphrased as 'our origin was protoplasm, our condition is misery, and we're going to blazes'. But one senses that his confusion between long-term cosmology and daily attitude was partly a pose; certainly, the razzles were nothing if not convivial. Obviously, shelter could go with extreme flexibility on ideology.

Nonetheless, Manson was important on the left – in a city where the main political cleavage was Orange versus Green. So it is all the more significant that persons politically so self-reliant (or at least unusual) could – as we will see when we return to Liverpool – easily become involved in an ironic hall of mirrors. At this time, strategic justifications were easily available for substituting strivings around friendship for directly political activity.

But wider factors were at work, too. Here, we move to broad plausibilities, some of these ruling class and some working class. The generations around 1900 saw, via all available channels and media, an unparalleled degree of projection (accurate or not) of a certain ruling-class personality-type as justification of a right both to rule at home and overseas, and to exemplify good character to the ruled. The Victorian and post-Victorian English gentleman has attracted a massive historiography. His chief forcing-houses – apart, importantly, from the army and the colonies – were sport and the public schools. The emphasis in the latter may, according to recent historians[8], have shifted from 'Godliness and Good Learning' via muscular Christianity to a Stoic version of Social Darwinism (associated, one might add, with a return of Christianity's uneasily repressed cousin Mithraism, an older cult of soldierly brotherliness); but these were nuances more important among purveyors than consumers. In schools and in youth organizations, the consumers were more or less captive, if sometimes rebelliously. Notoriously then as now, modern mass sport was much associated with public schools in origin and ethos. But socially, sport had no more than an ambiguous triumph among the 'lower orders': the latter shifted the cultural goalposts significantly, during decades and generations [9] – often, in effect, threatening to imitate their slightly earlier success within the socially more restricted arena of the Working Men's Clubs[10]. 'Class-reconciliation' might be a gentleman-sportsman's ideal when playing with men from across any felt divide, but it didn't always come about on their original terms.

The new – or, rather, modified – sports helped nurture a number of emphases relevant to considerations about friendship among people of every class. Two such, inseparably, were 'manliness' and 'chivalry'[11]. Via these, sport may possibly have had an effect so fundamental as to be easily overlooked – historiographically at least. Old sports – traditional forms of hurling and football in particular – had pitted against each other traditionally rival groups: neighbouring villages or opposite ends of town. Often, such contests were fought out over an arena – or rather terrain – of indefinite dimensions; usually and more important, they involved not so much a limited and therefore (theoretically) representative team, but almost anyone stably identifiable with the group represented. True, the team games which were brought into vogue during the late nineteenth century grew out of similar loyalties. But they soon developed beyond them, to involve team-sizes as rigidly fixed as pitch-sizes, more frequent games, far wider catchment areas and soon, most important, a hierarchy of competitions.

Thus, during any season, team games demanded repeated reprioritizations of loyalty: quite apart from individual transfers and other changes of allegiance, all the opponents in a joust at one level (say, club) were regularly transformed into part of the 'us' at another (say, international). Relevantly, here, most of the *Clarion*'s founding group – including Blatchford, Thompson and E. F. Fay (who, when not murdering his liver, was being promoted as the paper's cheerily deflationary model personality) – had more or less begun their journalistic careers in the environment of sporting papers. The main relevance of sport as something that accustomed those around it to reprioritizing their loyalties, is that switches of allegiance turned out to be very much on the agenda during the period. Here, individual Anglo-patriot-Irish rebels such as Erskine Childers or Sir Roger Casement are well known. (Indeed this syndrome was certainly to outlast the Great War: apart from the

Tory-turned-Labour MP, Sir Oswald Mosley, there was also to be Colonel L'Estrange Malone, the war-hero-turned-communist MP who was to do time for envisaging before a crowd in the Albert Hall the suspending of 'a few Churchills' from lamp-posts). Arguably, the syndrome was much more than individual: most suffragettes and most working-class and socialist activists – though not all – switched from militancy to enthusiastic or virtual patriotism during August 1914. During many years prior to that month, Blatchford had, though campaigning against what he saw as the German menace, retained his influence partly because even he could sometimes hesitate publicly between giving priority to the class, the international or potentially even the Ulster struggle. He was hardly alone. Notoriously, many army officers – not least his mutual admirer, Field Marshal Lord Roberts of Kandahar – shared his uncertainty over Ulster[12]. Such potential or actual switchings were obviously no mere effect of sport. But possibly sporting experience or merely atmosphere assisted many people's willingness to reprioritize their (political) world games[13].

The preceding paragraphs have alluded, mainly via sport, to more or less middle- and upper-class inputs into *circa* 1900 ideas about friendship. But, as remarked, the working-class hand in the modification of sports was powerful from the start. And, amid the working-class ingredients in both the sporting and *Clarion* brews, the more or less skilled working-class ones are merely the most traceable. To these we can now turn. Of these, a minor but insistent one was sectarianism. This had, for centuries, tended to begin (not necessarily among artisans either) with a level of sister- and brotherhood often so intimate, if not radical, as to infuriate the wider society (as with the early Society of Friends, or Quakers), but tended to gravitate within a generation or two towards some degree of artisanal or even middle-class respectability – occasionally accepting so high a degree of stabilization as quietly to give up or even (as the Muggletonians[14]) explicitly to renounce proselytization.

Sectarianism interacted unstably and often uneasily with broader artisan styles of friendship. Whether these originated more with the old guilds or with the solidarities of outlying manufacturing settlements, they entailed (amongst other features) conspicuous humiliation of the opponent and the backslider. They also involved suspicion of outsiders (often seen as linked to those two), and therefore tended to favour the use of initiations, pass-words or simply of in-group jargon. All these practices, particularly their rough-music aspect[15], occurred in areas far wider than the sphere of work (in so far as, prior to industrialization, the latter was at all clearly separated from the rest of life); but they were also carried into early trades unionism[16]. And many remained, as practices or mere proper-ways-of-doing-things, among some skilled trades unionists into the twentieth century.

Thus habit was important for determining the degree of ritualization of friendship: habit, and therefore origin. This can be gleaned if we compare co-operatives and friendly societies. By the end of the nineteenth century, these two movements had long had similar, often overlapping core memberships (skilled workers, more or less). Both, as their names imply, had originated in face-to-face solidarities but, by around 1900, many had become national and were racked by strenuous efforts to preserve their democratic rhythms[17]. Both were at the height of their power, or approaching it: the friendly societies have been argued[18] to have been, till 1911, on the point of dominating the provision of health to skilled workers and, increasingly, their families; the co-ops were, into the interwar years, even seen by small shopkeepers as threatening to obliterate them. Yet the societies were highly ritualized, the co-ops barely at all. This contrast becomes somewhat explicable when we remember that the first (or their grandparent organizations) had originally suffered under a legal environment that had been uncertain at best, whereas the second had not. But there is little surprise that, around 1900, Clarionettes – many of them young men who were at least entering the worlds of union and friendly society – were satirizing some working-class uses of internal jargon and in-jokes. *Clarion* satire tended to be inconsequential in both origin and content – whether the motto that there was 'no such place as Pudsey' or the recognition-shout of 'Boots!' answered by 'Spurs' – but no less solidarizing for that.

Mottoes and in-jokes that reached print in the *Clarion* became obviously as national as the *Clarion* itself was becoming. But there may also have been an undergrowth of local in-jokes – I say 'may' because these were very chancily recorded, when they were recorded at all. Perhaps significantly, our most striking example comes from one of the Pezzers, our instance of a small group of in-jokers. Our socialist stonemason (Fred Bower) had, during his childhood, led a gang associated with his (Protestant) school, while the not-yet-so-'Big' Jim Larkin had headed the Catholic opposition. During 1904 and employed on the foundations of Liverpool Cathedral, Bower approached his friend and old rival with a subversive scheme. Accordingly, Jim

> got a piece of tin and compressed a copy each of the *Clarion* and [Keir Hardie's] *Labour Leader* of June 24th, into it. I wrote the following short hurried note: 'To the Finders, Hail! We, the wage slaves employed on the erection of this cathedral, to be dedicated to the worship of the unemployed Jewish carpenter, hail ye! Within a stone's throw from here, human beings are housed in slums not fit for swine. This message, written on trust-produced paper, with trust-produced ink, is to tell ye how we of today are at the mercy of trusts . . . We can only sell our labour power . . . on their terms . . . In your day, thanks to the efforts of past and present agitators for economic freedom, . . . [you have] a happier existence. See to it, therefore, that ye, too, work for the betterment of *all* . . . Thus, and thus only shall come about the Kingdom of God or Good on Earth.
> Hail, Comrades, and Farewell,
> Yours sincerely,
> A Wage Slave'.

The next day, he duly built this into the foundations. Some time after, he asked Philip Snowden (Ramsay MacDonald's future Chancellor of the Exchequer, who happened to be visiting the city to deliver his ever popular sermon on 'the Christ that is to be') about publicity. Instead, Snowden strongly advised secrecy; and, until 1936 when Bower printed the story, those in the know (Manson, incidentally or not, among them) totalled ten. So, 22 days after the infiltration, 'King Edward VII duly did his bit, and laid the foundation stone over my document[19]. Of course, the possibility remains that Bower's story was itself an in-joke. But this would not lessen the importance of in-jokes.

A subverted foundation stone might, apparently, make a close comradeship all the closer. And it certainly has a simple logic. By contrast, many of the in-jokes and other devices which we have noted as presumably strengthening some types of association were logically hazy. They were no less so in their origin. Symbolically on the latter, Morris's motto (which opened this essay) became a favourite with most of the people discussed so far; Morris had placed this into the mouth of John Ball, whose role in stirring up the Peasants' Revolt of 1381 made him the greatest of his (Morris's) medieval English comrades. Morris undoubtedly saw himself as spreading the French Revolutionary ideals – not least that of *Fraternité*. But he also remained a romantic to the extent of couching much of his advocacy of a non-bureaucratic socialism in terms of an egalitarian version of pre-capitalist relations: feudal or – via his engagement with saga from the Old Norse to his own – even more archaic. His admiration for what he called paganism stemmed from reaction against capitalist, more than merely Christian, hypocrisy[20].

In him, such tensions between pre- and (he hoped) post-capitalist were sustainable. In others, they turned out not to be. Most of those who, particularly during the decades after his death in 1895, claimed to be his disciples made their socialist society of the future sound very much like an idealized Middle Ages. One of these was no less than Blatchford in his *Sorcery Shop* of 1907. There may, therefore, be some sense in which many *circa* 1900 socialists' 'delectable mountains' lay in a warm version of the past as much or more than in any discernible future. Consistently or not, the less discernible that future – let alone the way towards it – the stronger many people's need to arrange a foretaste of it in the here and now. But such foretastings themselves had an ambiguous status in relation to aim or strategy: arguments between Fellowship-as-recuperation for tired politicos (perhaps, therefore, as their springboard back into politics) and Fellowship-as-substitute for politics were much repeated over the years. And the longer you concentrated simply on having fun and being nice to each other, the nearer you became, in effect, merely a cheerier, less supervised equivalent of many more or less rival forms of association, from the Nonconformists' Pleasant Sunday Afternoons, to the would-be class-brotherhood of the public schools' slumland settlements.

Analogously, *Clarion* talk of helping lame dogs over stiles was, in effect, a kind of socialist chivalry. Those socialists who bestowed such help attributed their own comfier position – whether as middle-class, or simply as employed workers – not to the grace of God let alone of heredity (both of which Blatchford saw himself as having put paid to, the first to only mixed applause), but merely to the lottery of the capitalist system. Yet, within the often chivalry-obsessed society which Britain was around 1900, public schools were of course the most saturated area of all – with a chivalry unashamedly élitist. Obsessions with chivalry were admittedly hardly unique to Britain. But the educational and social influence of preparatory and public schools was one of the two major factors giving chivalry in Britain a peculiar many-sidedness – as we have seen exemplified in the area of sport. The other factor was a myth, which reinforced itself during generations, of the alleged Britishness of class-reconciliation and, therewith, of gradual improvement. The myth had been virtually continuous (though variably effective) since the late eighteenth century. The shock of the 1880s unemployment riots had merely spurred its most recent renewal.

Public school boys and men (or, in some all-female contexts, girls and women) were supposed to lead by a mix of example and proximity: the balance between the two varied. The trouble was, public schools themselves were repeatedly recognized as dangerously ambivalent. For, within and via them, though friends were often among the most lasting gains, friendship was the most fraught field of all. Whether the currently predominant ideal leant more towards 'good learning' or towards 'playing the game', there lay in wait behind same-sex friendships (and even more behind those involving teacher with pupil) the problem – alleged or real – which was repeatedly the subject of panic: namely 'immorality'. In its negotiation, there was at best ambiguous guidance to be derived from the twin influences at the heart of the official public-school ideology: the Bible and the classics. The public-school emphasis on sport and leadership (as prophylactic both against personal *over*-proximity and against class estrangement) was itself affected by the ambiguities it was supposed to combat. Such confusions, as well as various personal reactions to them, were at work both in the predilection of many upper- and middle-class male homosexuals (insofar as they can be stably defined) for working-class sexual partners and in the particular disgust generated by discoveries or re-discoveries of such practices via, for example, the 1889–90 Cleveland Street scandal. This disgust was there for the mobilizing against Oscar Wilde – as a seducer of young men of much lower status than that of his boyfriend, Lord Alfred Douglas – in 1895, or against Casement in 1916.

Such shocks must have increased the tension around ways of relating which, previously, may have involved many of these ambiguities without necessarily bringing them identifiably to the surface. It had been, we are told, 'widely accepted in Victorian society that strong and indeed often emotional relationships between men were normal.' Jeffrey Weeks sorts these relationships under a 'homosexual' heading, while himself giving various historical reasons for relativizing such labels[21]: late nineteenth-century moral panics were threatening to *make* such ambiguities dangerous. The threat was neatly summarized by one correspondent of Edward Carpenter: 'A few more cases like Oscar Wilde's and we should find the freedom of comradeship now possible to men permanently impaired.'[22]

Carpenter himself was a former clergyman of the Anglican church; a mystical socialist poet, smallholder and sandal-maker who kept open-house for heretics and left-wingers of all kinds – an institution built round his own cross-class and same-sex relationship which was seldom persecuted[23]. His correspondent was none other than W. T. Stead who, in 1885, had himself deliberately triggered a moral panic which – aside from its main focus (child prostitution) – had provided the occasion for a tightening of the law on homosexuality. True, Stead himself disapproved of his own by-product; but the point is that the unpredictability of moral panics was increased by their confused assumptions. And when Stead added that all this impairment of what he called 'comradeship between men' would be 'to the detriment of the race', he was merely using the fashionable vein of portentousness to underline how 'permanently' deep he felt the problem to be.

Legally, at least, the position of those women who deviated from approved forms of friendship was easier than that of men: as late as 1927, an attempt to introduce the first legislation against lesbian behaviour was to be voted down, on the argument that '999' out of 'every thousand women' – and also, allegedly, 100 per cent of Labour MPs – would be better left in ignorance of such possibilities[24].

True, there is a possibility that women's ignorance might have been exaggerated. But the more nineteenth-century upper- and middle-class women were socially confined, the more they sought friendship with each other, usually perhaps as solace but

172

sometimes also as a springboard. The century's later decades witnessed a flowering of female middle-class associativeness and, often in connection with this, assertiveness in a whole range of arenas from secondary and higher education to slum settlements and religious communities[25]. Strivings such as these certainly interacted with discussions about male and female sexuality. But they must often have seemed to relegate them to the background.

No doubt partly as a spin-off from them, a growing number of young women of respectable class were allowed by their families (after whatever dissensions) to live by themselves. A novel such as Isabella O. Ford's *On the Threshold* (1895) allows us to glimpse, reliably or not, a genteelly cramped bedsitterland, peopled by young women possessing the strength and leeway to live independently (if only just), plus the joint resources to employ one maid, however precariously. True, they confronted the lives of the mass of Londoners with an ignorance which a mere week of, say, settlement-work would have shattered. But their resourcefulness in dealing with landladies and occasional male pursuers was, one imagines, acquired more or less traumatically in the face of very different threats at girls' public schools. Similarly – and here even more relevantly – their experience of public-school religion may have boosted their ability to sit, with passably passive seriousness, through various drawing-room gatherings of world-improvers while avoiding obvious bad faith. More important still, their deepest loyalty remained to each other – or so they hoped: in other words, friendships were relevant not merely to strategies towards liberation but also to definitions of it.

This surfaced again in 1911, when the avoidance by some women of any involvement with men was attacked by some feminists as a barrier against women's sexual emancipation. 'Spinsters' were here denounced as part of the enemy (in effect, repression), irrespective of how hard they had tried to emancipate themselves according to *any* one or more of a range of definitions. Clearly, some feminists had, or believed they had, experienced one or more 'spinsters' as repressive. But both the virulence of the attack and the breadth of the target bedevilled the feminist movement; they also confirmed from an unexpected source the prejudice of many anti-feminists[26] and – for our purposes – underline how fraught a question friendship (or lack of it) could be.

Working-class women (the majority, obviously) left fewer records of friendship. This may perhaps have been a matter not simply of their lesser access to literacy and, of course, to spare time, but also of their lesser degree of privacy. Privacy could be a prison for middle-class women, but a luxury for working-class. Further, one lesson dinned into persons of any age within a working-class environment was that 'sticking together' (and to the motto of 'a friend in need') could easily become a prerequisite to survival. Certainly, while skilled men and a small minority of women had their unions and friendly societies, women anywhere in the working class needed informal neighbourhood networks (not these women's phrase, of course)[27]. These, though, were a matter of sheer solidarity, and not necessarily of any kind of friendship, however defined.

Friendship is thus interesting during these years for many reasons. The defence or improvement of character for socialism or for Empire or 'race' were key obsessions which criss-crossed on its terrain. This helped produce many richly ambiguous patterns. What, for example, did Blatchford think of his (political) comrade, Edward Carpenter's, lifestyle? As sage and poet, Carpenter attracted his admiration. But in morals, Blatchford was as conventional in his publicly expressed views as anyone. 'Manly' was as positive a word with him as with, say, any less left-wing defender of the Empire or, come to that, as with almost any skilled working-class male. And he waxed loud in his rejection of 'even the mildest forms of sensuality' as producing 'drunkenness and lust and kindred horrors.' In the name of what Shaw rightly denounced as his 'trumpery. . . little frame of red and blue ideals', he denounced Zola and rounded on Ibsen. Possibly, he accepted Carpenter's (and Ellis's) dubious dignifying of male homosexuals as simply born different: such a labelling could leave conventional categorizations of, for, and by, the majority, undisturbed, allowing him and Carpenter to confine their disagreements to a political field, which was treated as if peopled by heterosexuals alone.

Relevantly to the latter, *Clarion* institutions – and particularly the Cycling Clubs – were socially flexible. The Clarionettes, with their cult of informality (not least of that peculiarly informal vehicle, the bicycle), were not merely the group most open to anyone fit enough to cycle and in regular enough work to afford the smallish sum for an average machine, but were also, apparently, the socialist group least closed to women. Symbolically, Emmeline and (till his death) Dr Richard Pankhurst had been friends with Blatchford for some time before one or more of their daughters began cycling out with Clarionettes to Clarion Clubhouses. The Clarionette rhythms of commitment were often attractive to people exploring some dimensions of personal independence; so too, perhaps, was a lack of didacticism (though obviously this would have varied with individuals). That both qualities went with the socialist movement's most 'bicyclized' sector v as both cause and effect: cyclists could rendezvous in varying numbers and combinations, or peel – or pair – off. Thus they could vary the balance between enjoyment and agitation as spontaneously as they wished and as physical conditions permitted. The Clarionettes' success stemmed at least partly from making socialism fun for young people of indeterminate but unpretentious background, such as themselves: the frequent lack of manual working-class dominance – even where there was numerical predominance – was what scandalized some other socialists, and not merely the seeming lack of seriousness. Their cult of strategically vague political activism also involved a studied aversion to rules or regulations: the 'Pudsey' motto was occasionally trotted out for those who demanded such. Awares or not, Clarionettes often chimed with a very widespread self-image of the British as sincere because 'free-born': in their context, the rights of free-born Britons included freedom from deadly earnestness. (Gerald Newman is surely correct – if occasionally extreme – in tracing back to the mid-eighteenth century the protean workings of free-born Britishness[28].)

British images of friendship thus interacted frequently with the self-image of Britons. Hindsight tells us that socialist (and particularly *Clarion*) versions of this dialectic were to be undermined by disagreements as to whether Britons were free to refuse to fight when told, on overwhelming authority, that their freedom was externally endangered. Volunteers such as the Bradford Pals must surely have drunk the mud of Flanders with, some of them, experience as Clarionettes, and not merely as activists in the larger and more orthodox YMCAs or Pleasant

175

Sunday Afternoons. Before the Great War, British socialists had, awares or not, drawn succour from traditions of friendship and, therewith, of Britishness. During it, many were drawn into what one Clarionette unoriginally called 'the Great Adventure'; some others, outraged by it, were drawn closer together in networks of opposition, often against terrifying pressure[29]. After it, whether socialists, in many places, reknit their wartime schisms or not, the often more defensive struggles of the interwar period were never to restore friendship to a position where it could begin to substitute for political strategy. Instead, it played second fiddle – or should we say triangle?

NOTES

1 The best window on the Fellowship of the New Life and its influence remains W. H. G. Armytage (1961) *Heavens Below: Utopian Experiments in England, 1560–1960*, p. 327–47, London: Routledge & Kegan Paul.

2 On the Owenites generally, see J. F. C. Harrison (1969) *Robert Owen and the Owenites, the Quest for the New Moral World*, London: Routledge & Kegan Paul; on the Owenites and marriage, see Barbara Taylor (1983) *Eve and the New Jerusalem*, London: Virago; on the collectivist colonies, see Armytage (as in note 1) and Dennis Hardy (1979) *Alternative Communities in 19th century England*, London: Longman.

3 All statements about or around the *Clarion* are based on or taken from L. J. W. Barrow (1975) *The Socialism of Robert Blatchford and the 'Clarion' Newspaper, 1889–1918*, London D.Phil. thesis.

4 E.g. E. J. Hobsbawm (1964) *Labouring Men: Studies in the History of Labour*, chapter 14, London: Weidenfeld & Nicolson; R. Harrison (1987) 'Sidney and Beatrice Webb', in Carl Levy (ed.) *Socialism and the Intelligentsia, 1880–1914*, London: Routledge & Kegan Paul.

5 Stephen Yeo (1977) 'A new life: the religion of socialism in Britain, 1883–1896', *History Workshop*, issue 4, Autumn 1977.

6 R. T. Manson (1906) *Wayward Fancies*, transcribed by R.B. Suthers, Liverpool.

7 Fred Bower (1936) *Rolling Stonemason*, p. 155–160, London: Jonathan Cape; there is also the sketchier T. Joff (1915) *Coffee House Babble*, p. 25ff., Walton, Liverpool: the author.

8 E.g. Jeffrey Richards (1987) '"Passing the love of women": manly love and Victorian society', in J. A. Mangan and J. Walvin (eds) (1987) *Manliness and Morality*, Manchester: Manchester University Press.

9 See, exemplarily, Tony Mason (1980) *Association Football and English Society, 1863–1915*, Brighton: Harvester Press.

10 J. Taylor (1972) *From Self-Help to Glamour: The Working-man's Club, 1860–1972*, Oxford: History Workshop Pamphlet.

11 On the uses of 'chivalry', the outstanding book remains Mark Girouard (1981) *The Return to Camelot*, London: Yale University Press; see also J. A. Mangan (1981) *Athleticism in the Victorian and Edwardian Public School*, chapter 8, Cambridge: Cambridge University Press; and the Mangan and Walvin anthology (as in note 8).

12 Barrow, 1975 thesis (as note 3); for a highly erudite refusal to see the wood for the trees, see I. F. W. Beckett (ed.) (1986) *The Army and the Curragh Incident (n.b. Not Mutiny), 1914*, published, significantly, for the Army Records Society, London.

13 L. Barrow (1989) 'Solidarity with South African Workers in 1914', in R. Samuel and Gareth Stedman Jones (eds) *Patriotism*, London: Routledge.

14 Christopher Hill *et al.* (1983) *The World of the Muggletonians*, London: Temple Smith.

15 See C. R. Dobson (1980) *Masters and Journeymen*, London: Croom Helm; R. A. Leeson (1979) *Travelling Brothers*, London: Allen and Unwin; J. Rule (1981) *The Experience of Labour in 18th-century Industry*, London: Croom Helm; for a version of the longer term, R. N. Price (1980) *Masters, Unions and Men*, Cambridge: Cambridge University Press.

16 For a useful way into the significance for our understanding of the nineteenth century of the now voluminous historiography of eighteenth-century roughmusicking, see the two editorial essays in R. D. Storch (ed.) (1982) *Popular Culture and Custom in 19th-century England*, London: Croom Helm.

17 Particularly for the co-ops, see S. Yeo (1986) 'Socialism, the state and some oppositional Englishness', in R. Colls and P. Dodd (eds) *Englishness*, London: Croom Helm; similarly see 'Notes on three socialisms', in Carl Levy (1987) (as note 4).

18 If exaggeratedly by David Green (1985) *Working-Class Patients and the Medical Establishment*, London: St Martin's Press.

19 Bower (as note 7), pp. 121–3.

20 The richest introduction to Morris remains the 1977 version of E. P. Thompson, *William Morris, Romantic to Revolutionary*, London: Merlin Press.

21 Jeffrey Weeks (1981) *Sex, Politics and Society*, p. 109, London: Longman.

22 Weeks (1977) *Coming Out*, p. 21, London: Quartet Books.

23 For the main persecution, see Sheila Rowbotham and Jeffrey Weeks (1977) *Socialism and the New Life: the Personal and Sexual Politics of Edward Carpenter and Havelock Ellis*, pp. 81–91, London: Pluto Press.

24 Weeks (as in note 21), pp. 105ff; Weeks (as in note 22), pp. 106ff; Sheila Jeffreys (1985) *The Spinster and her Enemies*, pp. 113ff., London: Pandora.

25 Martha Vicinus (1985) *Independent Women*, London: Virago.

26 Jeffreys (as in note 24) pp. 93–100, 142–6, 173–8; Jeffreys (ed.) (1987) *The Sexuality Debates*, pp. 602–5, London: Routledge.

27 Ellen Ross (1983) 'Women's neighbourhood and sharing in London before the First World War', in *History Workshop* 15.
28 Gerald Newman (1987) *The Rise of English Nationalism*, London: Weidenfeld & Nicolson.
29 If, for example, we follow the first 117 pages of Sheila Rowbotham's (1986) *Friends of Alice Wheeldon*, London: Pluto.

INDEX